VEGETARIAN

Good Housekeeping

VEGETARIAN

MEATLESS RECIPES EVERYONE WILL LOVE

★ GOOD FOOD GUARANTEED ★

HEARST BOOKS
New York

HEARST BOOKS
New York

An Imprint of Sterling Publishing
387 Park Avenue South
New York, NY 10016

GOOD HOUSEKEEPING

Jane Francisco
EDITOR IN CHIEF

Courtney Murphy
CREATIVE DIRECTOR

Susan Westmoreland
FOOD DIRECTOR

Samantha B. Cassetty, MS, RD
NUTRITION DIRECTOR

Sharon Franke
KITCHEN APPLIANCES & FOOD TECHNOLOGY DIRECTOR

Cover Design: Chris Thompson and Yeon Kim
Interior Design: Yeon Kim

The Good Housekeeping Cookbook Seal guarantees that the recipes in this cookbook meet the strict standards of the Good Housekeeping Research Institute. The Institute has been a source of reliable information and a consumer advocate since 1900, and established its seal of approval in 1909. Every recipe has been triple-tested for ease, reliability, and great taste.

www.goodhousekeeping.com

For information about custom editions, special sales, and premium and corporate purchases, please contact Sterling Special Sales at 800-805-5489 or specialsales@sterlingpublishing.com.

ISBN 978-1-61837-152-2

Distributed in Canada by Sterling Publishing
c/o Canadian Manda Group, 165 Dufferin Street
Toronto, Ontario, Canada M6K 3H6
Distributed in the United Kingdom by GMC Distribution Services
Castle Place, 166 High Street, Lewes, East Sussex, England BN7 1XU
Distributed in Australia by Capricorn Link (Australia) Pty. Ltd.
P.O. Box 704, Windsor, NSW 2756, Australia

Manufactured in China

2 4 6 8 10 9 7 5 3 1

www.sterlingpublishing.com

CONTENTS

Warm French Lentil Salad
(page 80)

Foreword

I cook a lot of meatless dinners these days, finding that I'm not hungry for meat every night. Lucky for me, my inspiration comes directly from the Good Housekeeping Test Kitchen, where I get first-hand input on the best dishes to feed my family and to recommend for yours.

Like most Americans these days, I'm on the hunt for more dinners where whole grains, legumes, vegetables, and fruits take the forefront. It's not just that studies show a vegetarian-heavy diet can lower the risk for diabetes, heart disease, and other illnesses; vegetarian meals can also offer an affordable, tasty option for meals. And as long as the food is dive-in delicious, there are no complaints from my family.

Can a whole book on vegetarian cooking be real food for real families? Yes. This collection of more than 65 recipes will give you family-friendly weeknight choices that require no mysterious ingredients or complicated techniques. You'll find chapters on Classic Vegetarian, Soups and Stews, Lunch and Brunch, Main-Dish Salads, Quick Dinners, and One-Dish Meals—so whatever you're cooking for, we've got you covered.

Hearty breakfast options like Grown-Up Pizza Bagel (page 54) and Provençal Goat Cheese Tart (page 56) start the day for weekdays and brunch weekends alike. And forget about wimpy salads—you'll never look at salad the same way after feasting on our bulked-up options like White Bean Panzanella Salad (page 70) and Warm French Lentil Salad (page 80). Dinner options are expansive with flavorful takes on stir-fries, tacos, pizzas, and pasta like Cheeseless Black Bean Lasagna (page 26), Spaghetti with Roasted Sweet Potato (page 101), Skillet Vegetable Curry (page 94), and more. Whether you're new to the vegetarian scene or looking to add to your recipe repertoire, *Vegetarian* gives options to please everyone. And with these delicious triple-tested selections, we think you'll hear many exclamations of "Yum!"

SUSAN WESTMORELAND
Food Director, *Good Housekeeping*

Introduction

For generations, the mealtime mantra of mothers across America has been "Eat your vegetables!" Well, as usual, mom is right. So too are the health professionals who, for decades, have advocated a healthy diet of less meat and more fruits, vegetables, whole grains, low-fat or fat-free dairy products to help us live longer and better.

Americans have finally gotten the message. Tens of millions of people in the U.S. today have changed their eating habits to include more produce and grains and fewer animal products.

While you may not consider yourself a vegetarian, you probably do, in fact, eat a few meatless meals each week. Pancakes for brunch, yogurt and fruit for breakfast, an after-movie pizza with mushrooms and peppers, a quick lunch of vegetable-and-bean burritos, comforting mac-and-cheese casserole or take-out vegetable lo mein for dinner are all satisfying and nutritious fare, yet free of meat, fish, or poultry.

Types of Vegetarians

Vegetarians choose to eliminate animal products from their diets for any number of reasons—ethical, environmental, economic, or religious. But according to a recent Gallup Poll, the majority of people who choose to go meatless do so for health reasons. Vegetarians usually fall into one of these groups:

• The vegan, or total vegetarian, diet includes only foods from plant sources: fruits, vegetables, legumes (dried beans and peas), whole grains, seeds, and nuts.

• The lactovegetarian diet includes plant foods plus cheese and other dairy products.

• The ovo-lactovegetarian diet is the same as the lactovegetarian, but also includes eggs.

• The semi-vegetarian diet, which is frequently favored by those who are just easing into a vegetarian lifestyle or who want to add more meatless meals to their diet, does not include red meat but does include chicken and fish along with plant foods, dairy products, and eggs.

Eating Vegetarian

Good Housekeeping is not advocating for a vegetarian diet in *Vegetarian*. Rather, we assembled a collection of our favorite healthful, flavor-packed recipes because, like many of our readers, you want to add more nutritious meatless dishes to your family's meals. Perhaps you have a member of your family who is a vegetarian, or your child has just announced that he or she wants to give up all animal foods. Or you simply want to introduce more vegetables, fruits, whole grains, legumes, and low-fat products into your meals. In these pages, you'll find a veritable garden of tasty, appealing, meat-free dishes to please everyone at your table.

Like life, variety is the key to delicious vegetarian meals. Experiment with the many available grains, legumes, fruits, and vegetables and combine them with several of the vast array of herbs and spices to marry flavors and add punch. You'll discover that the possibilities are endless.

Nutritional Guidelines

The most important consideration for a nutritionally sound vegetarian diet is to consume a variety of foods and in sufficient amounts to meet the caloric and nutritional needs of each individual. If you are incorporating more meatless meals into your family's menus and fewer animal products, there are several nutrients that you need to focus on to be sure everyone is getting an adequate amount, particularly youngsters:

PROTEIN You don't need to consume meat, fish, or poultry to have enough protein in your diet. Protein needs can easily be met by eating a variety of plant foods. It is not necessary to include specific combinations of foods (such as rice and beans) in the same meal. A mixture of proteins from grains, legumes, seeds, and vegetables eaten throughout the day will provide enough of all the amino acids, the building blocks of protein, your body needs.

Some sources of protein for vegetarians: legumes (dried peas and beans), seeds, nuts and nut butters, soy protein, cheese, milk and yogurt, eggs, grains, and some vegetables.

IRON An integral part of hemoglobin which carries oxygen in the blood. Vegetarians who eliminate all meat, poultrys and seafood (the primary sources of iron) may be prone to an iron deficiency. Some sources of iron for vegetarians: legumes, dark green leafy vegetables (except spinach), enriched and whole-grain breads and cereals, nuts, and seeds. Cooking foods in cast-iron cookware can also boost their iron content.

CALCIUM The major building material for building bones and teeth.

Some sources of calcium for vegetarians: milk and milk products, dark green leafy vegetables (except spinach), calcium-fortified soy products, fortified juices, and cereals.

ZINC Essential for growth and development and proper functioning of the immune system. Some sources of zinc for vegetarians: legumes, wheat germ, whole grains, nuts, pumpkin and sunflower seeds, milk, and milk products.

VITAMIN B-12 Essential for formation of red blood cells and proper functioning of the nervous system. Animal products are the only natural food source of this vitamin.

Some sources of B-12 for vegetarians: milk and milk products, eggs, fortified foods, and supplements.

THE VEGETARIAN FOOD GROUPS

Adopting a healthful vegetarian or semi-vegetarian diet is as simple as choosing a variety of different foods daily from among each of the following seven categories. Try any of the suggested recipes.

BREADS AND GRAINS Choose whole or unrefined grain products whenever possible or use fortified or enriched cereals. Recipes: Mushroom-Barley Miso Soup, White Bean Panzanella Salad, and Couscous with Garbanzo Beans.

VEGETABLES AND FRUITS Always try to use the freshest produce you can get. When fresh is not available, opt first for frozen, then canned. Go for the deepest colors for the highest nutritional content: Most dark green leafy vegetables contain calcium and iron. Deep yellow and orange fruits and vegetables are good sources of beta carotene. Veggies and fruits are also rich in potassium, fiber, folic acid, and vitamin C. Recipes: Tomato and Orzo Salad, Ratatouille Rigatoni, Creamy Avocado Soup, and Lasagna Toss with Spinach and Ricotta.

BEANS, PEAS, SOY, AND OTHER LEGUMES Use beans, peas, and other legumes as a main dish or part of a meal often. They are excellent sources of protein, and also contribute zinc, calcium, and iron. Recipes: Southwestern Black Bean Burgers,

Red Bean and Collard Gumbo, Chickpea Mango Salad, and Falafel Sandwiches.

DAIRY PRODUCTS OR CALCIUM-RICH SUBSTITUTES If using dairy products, select reduced-fat, low-fat, or fat-free varieties whenever possible. Recipes: Tomato and Cheese Pie, Queso-Blanco Soft Tacos, and Eggplant Parmesan.

NUTS AND SEEDS Eat a variety of nuts and seeds as a snack, on fruit or vegetable salads, or in main dishes. They are a source of protein, zinc, and iron. Don't overdo—they are high in calories.

FATS Essential in any diet, but ideally, most fats should come from whole plant foods such as nuts, seeds, and avocado. Moderate amounts of plant oils such as olive, canola, and sesame are good choices for cooking or for salad dressings.

Toasted Ravioli Salad (page 73)

EGGS Because of their high cholesterol content, you may want to limit eggs to three or four a week or consider using commercial egg substitutes, which contain no cholesterol and can be used freely as a protein source. Recipes: Asparagus Omelet, Eggs in Spicy Tomato Sauce, Egg Salad Deluxe, and Mexican Potato Frittata.

PLANNING MEALS

The key to serving delicious vegetarian meals everyone will enjoy is to create dishes that include some of each food group and have a variety of tastes, colors, and textures.

If you're just beginning on the path to more meatless meals, you may find some resistance from the carnivores in your family. Understand that it will take some time for those who are used to thinking of vegetables as side dishes to see them as the main event. Ask everyone to contribute a list of his or her favorite foods. Many dishes that contain meat can be easily modified to make them vegetarian. Chili, stir-fries, and pasta dishes naturally lend themselves to meatless recipes.

In general, plan your meals around one main dish that is vegetable-, bean-, or grain-based. Then add the appropriate go-withs. For example, if your main course is a vegetable tart, accompany it with potato, grain, or corn for a nutritionally complete meal. With a main course of pasta, add a salad and whole-grain bread. A bean-and-vegetable casserole calls for a side of rice pilaf or other grain.

Tips for Busy People

Most of us spend our days on the go: at work, shuttling kids back and forth, shopping, doing chores. Preparing good, wholesome vegetarian meals for your family shouldn't be a burden. Here are a few shortcuts for healthier cooking.

1 Plan menus, make lists, then shop.

2 Make sure there are plenty of good-quality ingredients on hand for quick and/or last-minute meals such as pastas, canned beans and tomatoes, frozen vegetables, and cheeses.

3 Make two big casseroles or a double-batch of a one-pot dish that will feed your family for two nights. Serve with a salad and whole-grain bread.

4 On the weekend, do some basic prep work of foods that can be incorporated into meals during the week: Cook up some rice or other grain, make pasta sauce, or cook a pot of beans.

5 Get everyone involved in planning, shopping, and preparing meals. That way, they'll be more likely to eat and enjoy the meal. This approach is also a great way to get children started on healthy eating habits.

Cheeseless Black Bean
Lasagna (page 26)

1 | Classic Vegetarian

Chilis, quesadillas, pastas, and stir-fries are classic vegetarian recipe standbys you may already have in your repertoire. The Good Housekeeping twist to these favorites make sure the recipes are family-friendly as well as no-fuss, which is indicative of what this cookbook is about—hearty, easy recipes that the entire family will gobble up.

Beans offer a boost of protein to play center-stage in Vegetarian Chili, heightened with chunks of butternut squash, or mashed into homemade bean burgers. For the pasta route, the ratatouille triple-threat veggie combo of eggplant, tomatoes, and squash bring oomph to tomato sauce in Ratatouille Rigatoni. Slave less over the stovetop to whip up Pasta with No-Cook Tomato and Bocconcini Sauce. Any direction you go, we've got you covered.

VEGETARIAN **Chili**

Black soybeans, sold in convenient cans, have a better texture and flavor than the usual beige variety and add extra oomph to winter chili.

ACTIVE TIME: 30 MINUTES   **TOTAL TIME:** 50 MINUTES   **MAKES:** ABOUT 10 CUPS OR 6 MAIN-DISH SERVINGS

4 teaspoons olive oil

1 medium butternut squash (about 2 pounds), peeled and cut into 3/4-inch pieces

3 medium carrots, peeled and cut into 1/4-inch pieces

1 large onion (12 ounces), chopped

2 tablespoons chili powder

2 garlic cloves, crushed with garlic press

1 can (28 ounces) plum tomatoes

3 jalapeño chiles, seeded and minced

1 cup vegetable broth

1 tablespoon sugar

1/2 teaspoon salt

2 cans (15 ounces each) black soybeans, rinsed and drained

1 cup lightly packed fresh cilantro leaves, chopped

plain nonfat yogurt (optional)

1 In nonstick 5-quart Dutch oven or saucepot, heat 2 teaspoons oil over medium-high heat until hot. Add squash and cook, stirring occasionally, until golden, 8 to 10 minutes. Transfer squash to bowl; set aside.

2 In same Dutch oven, heat remaining 2 teaspoons oil. Add carrots and onion and cook, stirring occasionally, until golden, about 10 minutes. Stir in chili powder and garlic; cook, stirring, 1 minute longer.

3 Add tomatoes with their juice, jalapeños, broth, sugar, and salt; heat to boiling over medium-high heat, stirring to break up tomatoes with side of spoon. Stir in soybeans and squash; heat to boiling over medium-high heat. Reduce heat to low; cover and simmer until squash is tender, about 30 minutes.

4 Remove Dutch oven from heat; stir in cilantro. Serve chili with yogurt, if you like.

EACH SERVING: ABOUT 265 CALORIES, 15G PROTEIN, 40G CARBOHYDRATE, 6G TOTAL FAT (1G SATURATED), 0MG CHOLESTEROL, 480MG SODIUM.

TIP
Skip the optional dollop of yogurt to turn this recipe vegan.

SOUTHWESTERN
Black Bean Burgers

Easy weeknight meal strategy: make a double batch and freeze the uncooked burgers. Defrost 10 minutes, then cook, turning once, until heated through, about 12 minutes.

ACTIVE TIME: 10 MINUTES   **TOTAL TIME:** 16 MINUTES   **MAKES:** 4 SANDWICHES

1   can (15 to 19 ounces) black beans, rinsed and drained

2   tablespoons light mayonnaise

¼   cup packed fresh cilantro leaves, chopped

1   tablespoon plain dried bread crumbs

½   teaspoon ground cumin

½   teaspoon hot pepper sauce

nonstick cooking spray

1   cup loosely packed sliced lettuce

4   mini (4-inch) whole-wheat pitas, warmed

½   cup mild salsa

1   In large bowl, with potato masher or fork, mash beans with mayonnaise until almost smooth with some lumps. Stir in cilantro, bread crumbs, cumin, and hot pepper sauce until combined. With lightly floured hands, shape bean mixture into four 3-inch round patties. Spray both sides of each patty lightly with nonstick cooking spray.

2   Heat 10-inch skillet over medium heat until hot. Add patties and cook until lightly browned, about 3 minutes. With wide spatula, turn patties over, and cook until heated through, 3 minutes longer.

3   Arrange lettuce on pitas; top with burgers then salsa.

EACH SANDWICH: ABOUT 210 CALORIES, 13G PROTEIN, 42G CARBOHYDRATE, 3G TOTAL FAT (0G SATURATED), 0MG CHOLESTEROL, 715MG SODIUM.

> **TIP**
> Use vegan mayonnaise to turn this recipe entirely vegan.

RATATOUILLE **Rigatoni**

Traditional vegetables for ratatouille (a French stew eggplant, yellow summer squash, peppers, and onions) are roasted and turned into a healthy vegetarian sauce for rigatoni pasta.

ACTIVE TIME: 15 MINUTES   **TOTAL TIME:** 1 HOUR 15 MINUTES   **MAKES:** 6 MAIN-DISH SERVINGS

- 1 large (15 ounce) eggplant, trimmed and cut into ½-inch cubes
- 1 small onion (4 to 6 ounce) cut into ½-inch pieces
- 3 tablespoons extra-virgin olive oil
- ½ teaspoon salt
- ½ teaspoon ground black pepper
- 2 medium yellow summer squash, cut into ½-inch pieces
- 1 medium (4 to 6 ounces) red pepper, cut into ½-inch pieces
- 1 pound rigatoni pasta
- 1 can (14½ ounces) crushed tomatoes
- 1 garlic clove, crushed with garlic press
- ½ cup loosely packed fresh basil leaves, very thinly sliced
- ½ cup freshly grated Parmesan cheese

1 Preheat oven to 450°F. In 18 inch by 12 inch jelly-roll pan, combine eggplant, onion, 2 tablespoons oil, ¼ teaspoon salt, and ¼ teaspoon ground black pepper until well mixed. Spread in even layer. Roast vegetables 15 minutes.

2 Meanwhile, heat large covered saucepot of *salted water* to boiling on high. To pan with eggplant, add squash, pepper, remaining 1 tablespoon oil, ¼ teaspoon salt, and ¼ teaspoon ground black pepper. Stir gently until well mixed, then spread vegetables in even layer. Roast 25 to 30 minutes longer or until vegetables are very tender.

3 While vegetables are roasting, add pasta to boiling water and cook as label directs. Drain. In same saucepot, heat tomatoes and garlic to boiling on medium-high; cook 4 minutes or until slightly thickened. Remove saucepot from heat; add pasta and roasted vegetables and basil; stir until well combined.

4 Divide pasta and vegetable mixture among warm serving bowls. Sprinkle with grated Parmesan to serve.

....

EACH SERVING: ABOUT 455 CALORIES, 16G PROTEIN, 72G CARBOHYDRATE, 11G TOTAL FAT (3G SATURATED), 7MG CHOLESTEROL, 670MG SODIUM.

TIP

Nix the Parmesan in this pasta to make this into a vegan recipe.

EGGPLANT **Parmesan**

Does it get more comforting than a dish of Eggplant Parmesan? We don't think so. Note that the tomato sauce recipe makes 6 cups; use the leftover 2 cups in place of the marinara in the Ravioli-Green Bean Lasagna recipe on page 105.

ACTIVE TIME: 1 HOUR   TOTAL TIME: 2 HOURS PLUS STANDING   MAKES: 6 MAIN-DISH SERVINGS

TOMATO SAUCE

1   tablespoon olive oil

1   medium onion (8 ounces) finely chopped

4   garlic cloves, minced

2   cans (28 ounces each) whole tomatoes in puree

¼   cup tomato paste

1   teaspoon salt

¼   teaspoon ground black pepper

¼   cup loosely packed fresh basil leaves, chopped (optional)

EGGPLANT

3   medium eggplants (about 3 ¼ pounds)

2   tablespoons olive oil

½   teaspoon salt

BREAD-CRUMB TOPPING

2   teaspoons butter or margarine

2   slices firm white bread, coarsely grated

1   garlic clove, minced

2   ounces part-skim mozzarella cheese, shredded (½ cup)

2   tablespoons freshly grated Parmesan cheese

CHEESE FILLING

1   container (15 ounces) part-skim ricotta cheese

2   ounces part-skim mozzarella cheese, shredded (½ cup)

2   tablespoons freshly grated Parmesan cheese

¼   teaspoon ground black pepper

1 **Prepare Tomato Sauce:** In 4-quart saucepan, heat oil over medium heat until hot. Add onion and cook, stirring occasionally, until tender, about 8 minutes. Add garlic and cook 1 minute longer, stirring frequently.

2 Stir in tomatoes with their puree, tomato paste, salt, and pepper, breaking up tomatoes with side of spoon; heat to boiling over high heat. Reduce heat to low and simmer, uncovered, until the sauce thickens slightly, about 25 minutes. Stir in basil, if using. Makes about 6 cups.

3 **Prepare Eggplant:** Preheat oven to 450°F. Grease 2 large cookie sheets. Trim ends from eggplants and discard. Cut eggplants lengthwise into ½-inch-thick slices. Arrange slices in single layer on cookie sheets. Brush top of eggplant slices with oil and sprinkle with salt.

4 Bake eggplant slices 25 to 30 minutes or until tender and golden, rotating sheets and turning slices over halfway through cooking; remove eggplant from oven and turn oven control to 350°F.

5 Prepare Topping: In nonstick 10-inch skillet, melt butter over medium heat. Add grated bread and garlic, and cook, stirring occasionally, until lightly browned, about 7 minutes. Transfer to small bowl. Add mozzarella and Parmesan; toss until evenly mixed.

6 Prepare Filling: In medium bowl, mix ricotta, mozzarella, Parmesan, and pepper until blended.

7 Assemble the Casserole: Into 13" by 9" glass baking dish, evenly spoon 1 cup tomato sauce. Arrange half of eggplant, overlapping slices slightly, in baking dish. Top with 1 cup tomato sauce, then dollops of cheese filling. Top cheese with 1 cup tomato sauce, remaining eggplant, and remaining tomato sauce (about 1 cup). Sprinkle top with bread-crumb topping.

**8 Cover baking dish with foil and bake 15 minutes. Remove cover and bake until hot and bubbly, about 15 minutes longer. Let stand 10 minutes for easier serving.

EACH SERVING: ABOUT 380 CALORIES, 21G PROTEIN, 35G CARBOHYDRATE, 21G TOTAL FAT (10G SATURATED), 49MG CHOLESTEROL, 1,373MG SODIUM.

TIP

Select eggplants that are relatively heavy for their size, with skins that are smooth, taut, and shiny. Tan patches, scars, or bruises on the skin are signs of decay underneath. When you press an eggplant with your thumb, it should feel firm and bounce back. The fuzzy caps and stems should be green and free of decay and mold. Because eggplants are so highly perishable, buy no more than a day in advance.

CAESAR **Pasta Salad**

This colorful, veggie-rich pasta salad features a vegetarian Caesar dressing that's sure to please everyone—perfect for a spring or summer picnic.

ACTIVE TIME: 20 MINUTES   **TOTAL TIME:** 30 MINUTES   **MAKES:** 6 MAIN-DISH SERVINGS

und farfalle pasta

1   teaspoon grated lemon peel

¼   cup fresh lemon juice (from 2 large lemons)

¼   cup freshly grated Parmesan cheese, plus more for garnish

3   tablespoons light mayonnaise

3   tablespoons extra-virgin olive oil

2   garlic cloves, crushed with garlic press

1   teaspoon salt

1   teaspoon ground black pepper

1   pint multi-colored grape tomatoes, cut into halves

1   medium zucchini, grated

1   cup frozen peas, thawed

¼   cup packed fresh basil leaves, finely chopped, plus leaves for garnish

1 Heat large covered saucepot of *salted water* to boiling on high. Cook pasta as label directs.

2 Meanwhile, from lemon, grate peel and squeeze juice into large bowl. Whisk in Parmesan, mayonnaise, oil, garlic, pepper, and 1 teaspoon salt. Add tomatoes, zucchini, peas, basil, and cooked pasta; toss well. Serve warm or chilled. Can be refrigerated, covered, for up to 1 day. Garnish with Parmesan and basil.

EACH SERVING: ABOUT 415 CALORIES, 14G PROTEIN, 64G CARBOHYDRATE, 12G TOTAL FAT (2G SATURATED), 6MG CHOLESTEROL, 605MG SODIUM.

Pasta with No-Cook Tomato
AND BOCCONCINI SAUCE

Bocconcini (Italian for "little mouthfuls") are small balls of mozzarella that can be found packed in whey or water in gourmet shops and in the dairy case of some supermarkets. Sometimes they have been tossed with herbs such as basil and black and crushed red pepper. In this case, adjust the seasonings that are called for accordingly.

ACTIVE TIME: 20 MINUTES **TOTAL TIME:** 35 MINUTES PLUS STANDING **MAKES:** 6 MAIN-DISH SERVINGS

2   pints cherry tomatoes, each cut in half

½   cup loosely packed fresh flat-leaf parsley leaves, chopped

½   cup loosely packed fresh basil leaves, thinly sliced

¼   cup olive oil

1   teaspoon salt

¼   teaspoon ground black pepper

1   garlic clove, crushed with garlic press

1   package (16 ounces) penne or corkscrew pasta

12   ounces small mozzarella balls (bocconcini), each cut in half

1   In large serving bowl, stir cherry tomatoes, parsley, basil, oil, salt, pepper, and garlic. Let stand at room temperature at least 1 hour or up to 4 hours to blend flavors.

2   In large saucepot, cook pasta as label directs. Drain well.

3   Add pasta to tomato mixture; toss with bocconcini.

EACH SERVING: ABOUT 545 CALORIES, 21G PROTEIN, 64G CARBOHYDRATE, 23G TOTAL FAT (9G SATURATED), 44MG CHOLESTEROL, 540MG SODIUM.

CHEESELESS BLACK BEAN
Lasagna

This vegan delight is an ooey-gooey masterpiece even without the cheese. The secret is the tofu, which plumps up the lasagna with protein while still giving it a creamy goodness. For extra protein oomph, add the nutritional yeast. For photo, see page 12.

ACTIVE TIME: 25 MINUTES **TOTAL TIME:** 2 HOURS 30 MINUTES PLUS STANDING
MAKES: 8 MAIN-DISH SERVINGS

14 ounces extra-firm tofu, drained and patted dry

2 cans (15 ounces each) black beans, rinsed and drained

1 can (28 ounce) fire-roasted diced tomatoes

1 can (12 ounces) tomato paste

1 cup water

1 small onion (4 to 6 ounces) finely chopped

1 teaspoon dried oregano

¼ teaspoon garlic powder

2¼ teaspoons salt

5/8 teaspoon ground black pepper

¼ cup raw cashews

¼ cup nutritional yeast (optional)

3 tablespoons olive oil

2 tablespoons finely chopped fresh basil

8 ounces no-boil lasagna noodles

1 Place tofu between 4 paper towel sheets. Place heavy skillet on top for 1 hour, pressing down on tofu.

2 Meanwhile, preheat oven to 375°F. Into 4-quart saucepot, stir black beans, tomatoes, tomato paste, water, onion, oregano, garlic powder, 2 teaspoons salt, and ½ teaspoon pepper. Heat to boiling on medium-high, stirring often. Reduce heat to maintain simmer; simmer, uncovered, 30 minutes, stirring occasionally.

3 While sauce cooks, in food processor, pulse cashews until finely ground; transfer to large bowl, along with pressed tofu. With hands, crumble tofu until texture resembles ricotta cheese. Stir in yeast (if using), olive oil, basil, ¼ teaspoon salt, and ⅛ teaspoon pepper.

4 In 13" inch glass or ceramic baking dish, spread 1 cup tomato sauce and tofu mixture; repeat layering twice. Top with 1 cup sauce. Spread sauce to completely cover noodles. Bake, uncovered, 40 minutes or until noodles are tender. Let stand 15 minutes before serving.

EACH SERVING: ABOUT 340 CALORIES, 16G PROTEIN, 52G CARBOHYDRATE, 10G TOTAL FAT (1G SATURATED), 0MG CHOLESTEROL, 1,120MG SODIUM.

TOFU **Stir-Fry**

We call for a bag of broccoli flowerets to save cutting and trimming time. Choose extra-firm tofu; other types will fall apart while stir-frying. To serve, spoon the saucy mixture over quick-cooking brown rice, another time-saver.

ACTIVE TIME: 25 MINUTES   TOTAL TIME: 40 MINUTES   MAKES: 4 MAIN-DISH SERVINGS

3   tablespoons soy sauce

1   tablespoon brown sugar

1   tablespoon cornstarch

1   cup water

2   teaspoons vegetable oil

3   garlic cloves, crushed with garlic press

1   tablespoon peeled, grated fresh ginger

1/8 to 1/4 teaspoon crushed red pepper

1   bag (12 ounces) broccoli flowerets, cut into uniform pieces, if necessary

8   ounces shiitake mushrooms, stems removed and caps thinly sliced

1   medium red pepper, cut into 1-inch pieces

1   package (15 ounces) extra-firm tofu, patted dry and cut into 1-inch cubes

3   green onions, trimmed and thinly sliced

1 In small bowl, with wire whisk, mix soy sauce, brown sugar, cornstarch, and water until blended; set aside.

2 In deep nonstick 12-inch skillet, heat oil over medium-high heat until hot. Add garlic, ginger, and crushed red pepper and cook, stirring frequently (stir-frying), 30 seconds. Add broccoli, mushrooms, and red pepper and cook, covered, 8 minutes, stirring occasionally.

3 Add tofu and green onions and cook, uncovered, 2 minutes, stirring occasionally. Stir soy-sauce mixture to blend and add to skillet; heat to boiling. Boil, stirring, 1 minute.

EACH SERVING: ABOUT 225 CALORIES, 16G PROTEIN, 23G CARBOHYDRATE, 9G TOTAL FAT (1G SATURATED), 0MG CHOLESTEROL, 775MG SODIUM.

TIP

When stir-frying, make sure all ingredients are prepped and on standby before cooking.

QUESO-BLANCO Soft Tacos

These tacos are filled with queso blanco, a white cheese that's a bit firmer than mozzarella, so it holds its shape when melted. Don't confuse it with queso fresco, a crumbly fresh cow's milk cheese that's found in almost every Latin American country.

ACTIVE TIME: 20 MINUTES   TOTAL TIME: 25 MINUTES   MAKES: 4 MAIN-DISH SERVINGS

3 green onions, trimmed and thinly sliced

3 plum tomatoes, cut into ½-inch pieces

1 ripe avocado, peeled, pitted, and cut into ½-inch pieces

¼ small head romaine lettuce, thinly sliced (2 cups)

¼ cup loosely packed fresh cilantro leaves

1 cup mild or medium-hot salsa

1 package (12 ounces) queso blanco (Mexican frying cheese), cut into 12 slices

12 (6-inch) corn tortillas, warmed

1 lime, cut into 4 wedges

1 On platter, arrange green onions, tomatoes, avocado, lettuce, and cilantro. Pour salsa into serving bowl.

2 Heat nonstick 12-inch skillet over medium-high heat until hot. Add cheese and heat, turning once, until dark brown in spots, 2 to 3 minutes.

3 Place 1 cheese slice in each tortilla and fold in half. Serve tortillas immediately, adding green onions, tomatoes, avocado, lettuce, cilantro, salsa, and a squeeze of lime juice.

EACH SERVING: ABOUT 545 CALORIES, 26G PROTEIN, 49G CARBOHYDRATE, 29G TOTAL FAT (13G SATURATED), 60MG CHOLESTEROL, 1,300MG SODIUM.

MUSHROOM **Quesadillas**

Shave precious time when preparing this easy vegetarian meal by giving the mushrooms a quick, vigorous rinse with water before wiping them down with a paper towel.

ACTIVE TIME: 20 MINUTES   **TOTAL TIME:** 30 MINUTES   **MAKES:** 4 MAIN-DISH SERVINGS

- 2   tablespoons olive oil
- 1   pound portobello mushroom caps, cleaned and sliced
- 1   package (16 ounces) baby spinach
- ¼   teaspoon salt
- 2   green onions
- 1   romaine lettuce heart
- 8   (8-inches each) flour tortillas, soft-taco-size
- 4   ounces goat cheese, crumbled
- 1   cup salsa or salsa verde

1 Preheat oven to 425°F. Line 2 large cookie sheets with foil.

2 In 5- to 6-quart saucepot, heat oil on medium. Add mushrooms; cook 5 minutes or until tender, stirring occasionally. With slotted spoon, transfer to medium bowl; discard liquid. To same skillet, add spinach; cook 5 minutes, stirring frequently. Stir in salt. Transfer to bowl with mushrooms; discard liquid. While mushrooms and spinach cook, very thinly slice green onions and romaine.

3 Arrange 4 tortillas on cookie sheets; top with spinach mixture. Top with goat cheese, green onions, then remaining tortillas. Bake 10 to 12 minutes or until tortillas are golden and crisp, rotating cookie sheets between upper and lower racks halfway through baking. To serve, top with romaine and salsa.

EACH SERVING: ABOUT 525 CALORIES, 20G PROTEIN, 73G CARBOHYDRATE, 19G TOTAL FAT (6G SATURATED), 73MG CHOLESTEROL, 1110MG SODIUM.

Tomato Soup with Quesadilla Dippers (page 44)

2 Soups & Stews

For busy cooks with families on the go, soups and stews are a godsend. They need minimal prep work, usually just chopping vegetables and measuring the required amounts of liquid, grains, herbs, and spices that go into the pot.

So what will it be tonight? How about the comfort of everyone's favorite bistro classics, French Onion Soup or Broccoli and Cheddar Soup? Savor the flavors of the Old South with a vegetarian take on a classic with Red Bean and Collard Gumbo. If the exotic appeals to you, try the Caribbean Black Bean Soup or Curried Sweet-Potato and Lentil Soup, redolent with Indian spices.

And lest you think soups and stews are winter-only meals, while you're firing up the outdoor grill, sit down to the refreshing Tomato Soup (paired with quesadilla dippers) and the chilled indulgence of Creamy Avocado Soup.

Curried Sweet-Potato
AND LENTIL SOUP

This thick and hearty soup is bursting with flavors from curry powder, ginger, cumin, and more. Get it going, then call a friend or spend some time with the kids while it simmers.

ACTIVE TIME: 15 MINUTES **TOTAL TIME:** 1 HOUR 30 MINUTES **MAKES:** 8 MAIN-DISH SERVINGS

2 tablespoons butter or margarine

2 medium sweet potatoes (about 12 ounces each), peeled and cut into ½-inch chunks

2 large stalks celery, cut into ¼-inch pieces

1 large onion (12 ounces), cut into ¼-inch pieces

1 garlic clove, minced

1 tablespoon curry powder

1 tablespoon grated, peeled fresh ginger

1 teaspoon ground cumin

1 teaspoon ground coriander

1 teaspoon salt

⅛ teaspoon ground red pepper (cayenne)

2 cans (14 ½ ounces each) vegetable broth (3 ½ cups)

1 package (16 ounces) dry lentils, rinsed and picked through

6 cups water

yogurt, toasted coconut, and lime wedges (optional)

1 In 6-quart Dutch oven, melt butter over medium heat. Add the sweet potatoes, celery, and onion and cook, stirring occasionally, until onion is tender, about 10 minutes. Add garlic, curry powder, ginger, cumin, coriander, salt, and ground red pepper; cook, stirring, 1 minute.

2 To vegetables in Dutch oven, add broth, lentils, and water; heat to boiling over high heat. Reduce heat to low; cover and simmer, stirring occasionally, until lentils are tender, 40 to 45 minutes. Serve with yogurt, toasted coconut, and lime wedges, if you like.

EACH SERVING WITHOUT YOGURT, COCONUT, AND LIME: ABOUT 295 CALORIES, 15G PROTEIN, 15G CARBOHYDRATE, 5G TOTAL FAT (2G SATURATED), 8MG CHOLESTEROL, 646MG SODIUM.

TIP

To make this soup vegan, swap the butter for olive oil.

Hot and Sour SOUP

We streamlined seasonings to help get this popular Asian soup on the table in record time—without sacrificing the great taste.

ACTIVE TIME: 10 MINUTES   **TOTAL TIME:** 30 MINUTES   **MAKES:** 4 MAIN-DISH SERVINGS

1 tablespoon vegetable oil

4 ounces shiitake mushrooms, stems removed and caps thinly sliced

3 tablespoons reduced-sodium soy sauce

1 package (15 to 16 ounces) extra-firm tofu, drained, patted dry, and cut into 1-inch cubes

2 tablespoons cornstarch

1 container (32 ounces) vegetable broth (4 cups)

3 tablespoons seasoned rice vinegar

2 tablespoons grated, peeled fresh ginger

1 tablespoon Worcestershire sauce

½ teaspoon Asian sesame oil

¼ teaspoon ground red pepper (cayenne)

2 large eggs, beaten

2 green onions, trimmed and sliced

1 In nonstick 5-quart saucepot, heat vegetable oil over medium-high heat until hot. Add mushrooms, soy sauce, and tofu and cook, gently stirring often, until liquid has evaporated, about 5 minutes.

2 In cup, with fork, blend cornstarch and ¼ *cup water* until smooth; set aside. Add broth and ¾ *cup water* to tofu mixture; heat to boiling. Stir in cornstarch mixture and boil, stirring, 30 seconds. Reduce heat to medium-low; add vinegar, ginger, Worcestershire, sesame oil, and pepper and simmer 5 minutes.

3 Remove saucepot from heat. In a thin, steady stream, slowly pour beaten eggs into soup around side of saucepot. Carefully stir soup once in circular motion to separate egg into strands. Sprinkle with green onions.

EACH SERVING: ABOUT 280 CALORIES, 18G PROTEIN, 17G CARBOHYDRATE, 15G TOTAL FAT (3G SATURATED), 106MG CHOLESTEROL, 1,790MG SODIUM.

TIP

To brown, tofu should be dry. Wrap in paper towels and set it on a plate. Cover with a second plate; place a heavy can on top and let drain fifteen minutes. Discard towels.

MUSHROOM-BARLEY Miso Soup

Simmering shiitake mushrooms and barley in a miso broth brings new depth to the classic mushroom and barley combo. Just note to never boil miso; its delicate flavor and nutrients will be destroyed by the high heat.

ACTIVE TIME: 20 MINUTES   TOTAL TIME: 1 HOUR 20 MINUTES   MAKES: 6 MAIN-DISH SERVINGS

1   package (1 ounce) dried shiitake mushrooms

1   tablespoon olive oil

3   medium carrots, peeled and cut into ¼-inch pieces

1   medium onion (8 ounces) chopped

2   garlic cloves, minced

1   tablespoon grated, peeled fresh ginger

½   cup pearl barley

½   teaspoon salt

¼   teaspoon ground black pepper

1½ pounds bok choy, trimmed and chopped

6   tablespoons dark red miso

1   tablespoon brown sugar

1   In 2-quart saucepan, heat *4 cups water* to boiling over high heat. Remove saucepan from heat; add dried shiitake mushrooms and let stand until softened, about 15 minutes. With slotted spoon, remove mushrooms. Rinse to remove any grit; drain on paper towels. Cut stems from mushrooms and discard; thinly slice caps. Strain soaking liquid through sieve lined with paper towels into 4-cup glass measuring cup. Add enough water to liquid in cup to equal 4 cups and set aside.

2   In nonstick 5-quart Dutch oven, heat oil over medium heat until hot. Add carrots, onion, and mushrooms and cook, stirring occasionally, until vegetables are tender, about 15 minutes. Add garlic and ginger and cook 1 minute longer.

3   Add barley, salt, pepper, reserved mushroom liquid, and an additional *4 cups water*; heat to boiling over medium-high heat. Reduce heat to low; cover and simmer until barley is tender, about 40 minutes.

4   Add bok choy; heat to boiling over medium-high heat. Reduce heat to low and simmer, uncovered, until bok choy is tender-crisp and wilted, 5 to 7 minutes, stirring occasionally.

5   With ladle, transfer ½ cup broth from soup to small bowl. Add miso and brown sugar to broth and stir until smooth paste forms.

6   Remove Dutch oven from heat; stir in miso mixture.

EACH SERVING: ABOUT 170 CALORIES, 7G PROTEIN, 29G CARBOHYDRATE, 4G TOTAL FAT (0G SATURATED), 0MG CHOLESTEROL, 985MG SODIUM.

TIP

Red miso, typically ranging in color from red to brown, is usually made from soybeans fermented with grains. The most common of the misos, it has a heartier flavor than white or yellow miso.

GINGERY CHICKPEA AND
Tomato Stew

The chickpea stew can be prepared up to 2 days ahead; transfer to an airtight container and refrigerate. The cilantro yogurt and rice are best prepared just before serving.

ACTIVE TIME: 15 MINUTES   **TOTAL TIME:** 40 MINUTES   **MAKES:** 4 MAIN-DISH SERVINGS

2   tablespoons vegetable oil

1   (1 pound) jumbo onion, chopped

2   garlic cloves, crushed with garlic press

1   cup basmati rice

1   cup low-fat plain yogurt

¼   cup packed fresh cilantro leaves, finely chopped

2   teaspoons ground cumin

1   teaspoon ground coriander

¼   teaspoon ground red pepper (cayenne)

1   can (28 ounces) diced tomatoes

2   tablespoons fresh lemon juice

1   tablespoon grated, peeled fresh ginger

3   cups cooked garbanzo beans, or 2 cans (15 ounces each) low-sodium garbanzo beans

½   cup water

1½ teaspoons sugar

¼   teaspoon salt

pappadums, Indian flatbreads, for serving (optional)

1   In 5- to 6-quart saucepot, heat oil on medium until hot. Add onion and garlic. Cook 10 minutes or until golden and tender, stirring occasionally.

2   Meanwhile, cook rice as label directs. In small bowl, combine yogurt and cilantro. Cover and refrigerate cilantro yogurt until ready to serve.

3   To saucepot with onion, add cumin, coriander, and ground red pepper. Cook 1 minute or until fragrant, stirring. Add tomatoes, lemon juice, and ginger. Heat to boiling, then stir in garbanzo beans and water. Simmer 15 to 20 minutes or until sauce thickens, mashing a few beans and stirring occasionally. Stir in sugar and salt.

4   Divide rice among dinner plates. Top with bean mixture and yogurt. Serve with pappadums, if you like.

EACH SERVING: ABOUT 580 CALORIES, 21G PROTEIN, 95G CARBOHYDRATE, 12G TOTAL FAT (2G SATURATED), 4MG CHOLESTEROL, 660MG SODIUM.

CREAMY **Avocado Soup**

This cool, creamy soup takes only minutes to whip up in the blender, but the combination of rich avocado and sour cream give it a luxurious texture. It's a needed indulgence on hot summer days especially.

ACTIVE TIME: 10 MINUTES   **TOTAL TIME:** 90 MINUTES   **MAKES:** 4 SERVINGS

1   avocado, pitted and peeled

1   cup sour cream

1   cup cold water

¾   cup salsa verde

¼   cup packed fresh cilantro leaves, plus more for garnish

½   teaspoon salt

½   teaspoon ground black pepper

roasted salted pumpkin seeds, for garnish

1   In blender, puree avocado, sour cream, water, salsa verde, ¼ cup packed fresh cilantro leaves, salt, and pepper until smooth.

2   Cover; refrigerate until cold. Divide among 4 bowls; sprinkle with roasted, salted pumpkin seeds and cilantro.

EACH SERVING: ABOUT 197 CALORIES, 2G PROTEIN, 9G CARBOHYDRATE, 18G TOTAL FAT (6G SATURATED), 25MG CHOLESTEROL, 678MG SODIUM.

French Onion SOUP

Slowly cooked onions add sweet, caramelized flavor to this classic. If you double the recipe, be sure to cook the onions in two skillets.

ACTIVE TIME: 15 MINUTES   TOTAL TIME: 2 HOURS   MAKES: 4 MAIN-DISH SERVINGS

3   tablespoons butter or margarine

7   medium onions (about 2 ½ pounds), each cut lengthwise in half and thinly sliced

¼   teaspoon salt

4   cups water

1   can (14 ½ ounces) vegetable broth (1 ¾ cups)

¼   teaspoon dried thyme

4   slices (½ inch thick) French bread

4   ounces Gruyère or Swiss cheese, shredded (1 cup)

1 In 12-inch skillet, melt butter over medium heat. Add onions and salt and cook, stirring occasionally, until onions are very tender and begin to caramelize, about 45 minutes. Reduce heat to low; cook, stirring often, until onions are deep golden brown, about 15 minutes longer.

2 Transfer onions to 3-quart saucepan. Add ½ cup water to skillet; heat to boiling over high heat, stirring until browned bits are loosened from bottom of pan. Pour into saucepan with onions. Add broth, thyme, and remaining water; heat to boiling over high heat. Reduce heat to low; cover and simmer until onions are very tender, about 30 minutes.

3 Meanwhile, preheat oven to 450°F. Place bread slices on small cookie sheet; bake until lightly toasted, about 5 minutes.

4 Place four 2½-cup oven-safe bowls in 15½" by 10½" jelly-roll pan. Spoon onion soup into bowls; top with toasted bread, pressing toast lightly into soup. Sprinkle toast with cheese. Bake until cheese melts and begins to brown, 12 to 15 minutes.

EACH SERVING: ABOUT 375 CALORIES, 15G PROTEIN, 38G CARBOHYDRATE, 23G TOTAL FAT (11G SATURATED), 54MG CHOLESTEROL, 808MG SODIUM.

Tomato Soup WITH
QUESADILLA DIPPERS

Grilling some of the vegetables for the tomato soup gives it a mellow, slightly smoky flavor. If you'd like a little more zip, you can leave the seeds and ribs in the jalapeño before blending. For photo, see page 32.

ACTIVE TIME: 25 MINUTES   TOTAL TIME: 45 MINUTES   MAKES: 4 MAIN-DISH SERVINGS

1 small onion, cut crosswise into ½-inch-thick slices

1 small jalapeño chile

2 garlic cloves, not peeled

2 pounds ripe tomatoes (about 4 large)

1 seedless cucumber (English), peeled and cut in half

¼ cup fresh lime juice (from 2 to 3 limes)

½ teaspoon salt

6 ounces shredded Monterey Jack cheese

12 corn tortillas

1 can no-salt-added pinto beans, rinsed and drained

¼ cup loosely packed fresh cilantro leaves

1 avocado, chopped

1 Prepare outdoor grill for direct grilling on medium-high.

2 Place onion, jalapeño, garlic, and tomatoes on hot grill grate. Cook tomatoes about 8 minutes or until skin blisters and splits, turning over once. Cook onion, jalapeño, and garlic 12 minutes or until charred and softened, turning over once. Reduce grill heat to medium-low.

3 Remove and discard peel from tomatoes and garlic; transfer to blender. Discard seeds and ribs from jalapeño; add to blender along with onion, half of cucumber, lime juice, and salt. Puree until smooth. Transfer to bowl; cover, set in larger bowl filled with ice and water, and refrigerate until cold, about 10 minutes. Or, cover soup and refrigerate at least 4 hours. Finely chop remaining cucumber.

4 Meanwhile, divide half of cheese among 6 tortillas. Top with beans, half of cilantro, remaining cheese, and remaining tortillas. Carefully transfer to grill; cook quesadillas 6 minutes or until cheese melts, turning over once.

5 Cut quesadillas into wedges. Divide soup among 4 bowls. Top with avocado, remaining cucumber, and cilantro. Serve with quesadillas.

EACH SERVING: ABOUT 515 CALORIES, 23G PROTEIN, 64G CARBOHYDRATE, 21G TOTAL FAT (9G SATURATED), 38MG CHOLESTEROL, 580MG SODIUM.

CHUNKY VEGETABLE **Chowder**

You can vary the assortment of fall vegetables in this hearty, vegan soup. Swap in fennel for celery, butternut squash for parsnips, a handful of fresh basil for the thyme.

ACTIVE TIME: 20 MINUTES　　TOTAL TIME: 50 MINUTES　　MAKES: 6 MAIN-DISH SERVINGS

2　tablespoons olive oil

1　jumbo onion (1 pound), cut into ¼-inch pieces

12　ounces red potatoes, not peeled and cut into ½-inch pieces

3　medium carrots, peeled and cut into ¼-inch pieces

2　medium parsnips (about 8 ounces), peeled and cut into ¼-inch pieces

2　medium stalks celery, cut into ¼-inch pieces

2　garlic cloves, crushed with garlic press

1　can (14 ½ ounces) vegetable broth (1 ¾ cups)

¾　teaspoon salt

¼　teaspoon dried thyme

4½ cups water

1　package (10 ounces) frozen Fordhook lima beans

12　ounces escarole or Swiss chard, trimmed and coarsely chopped

1 In nonstick 5- to 6-quart saucepot or Dutch oven, heat oil over medium-high heat until very hot. Add onion, potatoes, carrots, parsnips, celery, and garlic and cook, stirring occasionally, until vegetables are lightly browned, 15 minutes.

2 Add broth, salt, thyme, and water; heat to boiling over medium-high heat. Stir in lima beans and escarole; heat to boiling. Reduce heat to low; cover and simmer until vegetables are tender, about 10 minutes.

EACH SERVING: ABOUT 220 CALORIES, 7G PROTEIN, 39G CARBOHYDRATE, 5G TOTAL FAT (1G SATURATED), 0MG CHOLESTEROL, 675MG SODIUM.

CARIBBEAN Black Bean Soup

Our new take on black bean soup is made with allspice, thyme, and brown sugar for authentic island flair. Chunks of hearty sweet potato increase the heartiness of this dish.

ACTIVE TIME: 45 MINUTES   TOTAL TIME: 3 HOURS 15 MINUTES PLUS SOAKING BEANS
MAKES: 6 MAIN-DISH SERVINGS

1   pound dry black beans

2   tablespoons vegetable oil

2   medium red onions, chopped

4   jalapeño chiles, seeded and minced

2   tablespoons minced, peeled fresh ginger

4   garlic cloves, minced

½   teaspoon ground allspice

½   teaspoon dried thyme

8   cups water

2   medium sweet potatoes (about 12 ounces each), peeled and cut into ¾-inch pieces

1   tablespoon dark brown sugar

2   teaspoons salt

1   bunch green onions, trimmed and thinly sliced

1   cup lightly packed fresh cilantro leaves, chopped

2   limes, cut into wedges (optional)

1   Place beans in colander and pick through, discarding any stones or debris. Rinse beans with cold running water and drain. Transfer beans to large bowl. Add enough water to cover by 2 inches. Cover and let stand at room temperature overnight. (Or, in 5-quart Dutch oven or saucepot, combine beans and enough water to cover by 2 inches; heat to boiling over high heat. Boil 2 minutes. Remove from heat; cover and let stand 1 hour.) Drain and rinse beans.

2   In 6-quart saucepot, heat vegetable oil over medium heat until hot. Add onions and cook, stirring occasionally, until tender, about 10 minutes. Add jalapeños, ginger, garlic, allspice, and thyme and cook, stirring, 3 minutes.

3   Add beans and water; heat to boiling over high heat. Reduce heat to low; cover and simmer 1 hour 30 minutes.

4   Add sweet potatoes, brown sugar, and salt; heat to boiling over high heat. Reduce heat to low; cover and simmer until beans and sweet potatoes are tender, about 30 minutes longer.

5   Transfer 1 cup bean mixture to blender; cover, with center part of cover removed to let steam escape, and puree until smooth. Return to saucepot. Stir in green onions and cilantro. Serve with lime wedges, if you like.

EACH SERVING: ABOUT 390 CALORIES, 17G PROTEIN, 70G CARBOHYDRATE, 6G TOTAL FAT (1G SATURATED), 0MG CHOLESTEROL, 705MG SODIUM.

RED BEAN AND COLLARD **Gumbo**

Gumbo is traditionally made with a variety of meats and shellfish, but you're not likely to be disappointed with this all-vegetable version that is bulked up with greens.

ACTIVE TIME: 20 MINUTES   **TOTAL TIME:** 50 MINUTES   **MAKES:** 4 MAIN-DISH SERVINGS

¼ cup all-purpose flour

1 tablespoon olive oil

1 medium onion (8 ounces) thinly sliced

1 medium red pepper, cut into ½-inch pieces

1 large stalk celery, thinly sliced

2 garlic cloves, crushed with garlic press

½ teaspoon salt

¼ teaspoon ground red pepper (cayenne)

¼ teaspoon dried thyme

¼ teaspoon ground allspice

1 can (14 ½ ounces) vegetable broth (1¾ cups)

3 cups water

1 bunch collard greens (about 1¼ pounds), tough stems trimmed and leaves coarsely chopped

2 cans (15 to 19 ounces each) small red beans, rinsed and drained

1 In dry nonstick 5-to 6-quart saucepot, toast flour over medium heat, stirring frequently, until pale golden, about 5 minutes. Transfer flour to medium bowl; set aside.

2 In same saucepot, heat oil over medium-high heat until hot. Add onion, red pepper, and celery and cook, stirring occasionally, until vegetables are tender-crisp, about 10 minutes. Add garlic, salt, ground red pepper, thyme, and allspice and cook, stirring, 2 minutes.

3 Whisk broth into toasted flour until blended. Stir broth mixture and water into vegetables in saucepot; heat to boiling over medium-high heat. Add collard greens, stirring until wilted; stir in beans. Heat gumbo to boiling. Reduce heat to medium-low; cover and simmer until greens are tender, about 10 minutes.

EACH SERVING: ABOUT 330 CALORIES, 17G PROTEIN, 58G CARBOHYDRATE, 6G TOTAL FAT (1G SATURATED), 0MG CHOLESTEROL, 1,190MG SODIUM.

BROCCOLI AND **Cheddar Soup**

For a satisfying meal, serve this rich soup with an artisanal multigrain bread and a crisp salad. Use a blender—not a food processor—for an extra-smooth texture.

ACTIVE TIME: 35 MINUTES   TOTAL TIME: 1 HOUR   MAKES: 4 MAIN-DISH SERVINGS

1   tablespoon olive oil

1   medium onion (8 ounces) chopped

¼   cup all-purpose flour

½   teaspoon salt

¼   teaspoon dried thyme

⅛   teaspoon ground nutmeg

¼   teaspoon ground black pepper, plus more for garnish

2   cups reduced-fat milk (2%)

1   can (14½ ounces) vegetable broth (1¾ cups)

1½ cups water

1   large bunch (1 ½ pounds) broccoli, trimmed and cut into 1-inch pieces (including stems)

1½ cups shredded sharp Cheddar cheese (6 ounces)

1 In 4-quart saucepan, heat oil over medium heat until hot. Add onion and cook, stirring occasionally, until golden, about 10 minutes. Stir in flour, salt, thyme, nutmeg, and pepper; cook, stirring frequently, 2 minutes.

2 Gradually stir in milk, broth, and water. Add broccoli and heat to boiling over high heat. Reduce heat to low; cover and simmer until broccoli is tender, about 10 minutes.

3 Spoon one-third of mixture into blender; cover, with center part of cover removed to let steam escape, and puree until very smooth. Pour into large bowl. Repeat with remaining batches.

4 Return the soup to saucepan; heat to boiling over high heat, stirring occasionally. Remove saucepan from heat; stir in cheese until melted and smooth. Sprinkle each serving with ground black pepper.

EACH SERVING: ABOUT 362 CALORIES, 24G PROTEIN, 26G CARBOHYDRATE, 22G TOTAL FAT (12G SATURATED), 52MG CHOLESTEROL, 934MG SODIUM.

Provençial Goat Cheese Tart (page 56)

3 Lunch & Brunch

When you think brunch, the first thing that comes to mind are eggs, one of nature's most nutrient-rich and versatile foods. Not only are eggs an inexpensive protein source, they provide a tasty base for using up leftover veggies, cheese, and herbs.

In the pages that follow, you'll find eggs baked in pies, tarts, frittatas, and quiches; scrambled and in omelets; poached in a spicy tomato sauce. And for those weekends when you're having house guests, nothing beats make-ahead masterpieces like the Spring Onion, Spinach, and Pecorino Frittata or Greens and Ricotta Pie.

There are non-egg dishes to choose from, too. They can be as simple as substantial sandwiches—like a PTL Sandwich using the meaty portobello mushroom, homemade falafel stuffed into pitas, or focaccia stuffed with marinated artichokes and roasted red peppers.

SPRING ONION, SPINACH, AND PECORINO **Frittata**

For a less assertive flavor, substitute Parmigiano-Reggiano for the Pecorino Romano or use a combination of the two for a more complex flavor.

ACTIVE TIME: 30 MINUTES   **TOTAL TIME:** 40 MINUTES   **MAKES:** 4 MAIN-DISH SERVINGS

2 spring onions with tops (about 12 ounces), or 1 large (12 ounces) sweet onion

2 teaspoons olive oil

1 bag (5 to 6 ounces) baby spinach

8 large eggs

¼ cup freshly grated Pecorino Romano cheese

¼ cup water

½ teaspoon salt

¼ teaspoon ground black pepper

1 Preheat oven to 425°F. Trim tough green leaves from top of spring onions. Cut stems crosswise into ¼-inch-thick slices. Cut each onion bulb in half and thinly slice.

2 In oven-safe nonstick 12-inch skillet (if skillet is not oven-safe, wrap handle with double layer of foil), heat oil over medium heat until hot. Add sliced onions and stems and cook, stirring occasionally, until soft and golden brown, about 10 minutes. Stir in spinach and cook, stirring constantly, just until wilted, about 1 minute. Spread onion mixture evenly in skillet; remove skillet from heat.

3 In medium bowl with wire whisk, beat eggs, Pecorino Romano, water, salt, and pepper until blended. Carefully pour egg mixture over onion mixture; do not stir. Return skillet to medium-high heat and cook until egg mixture begins to set around the edge, 2 to 3 minutes.

4 Place skillet in oven; bake until frittata is set, 8 to 10 minutes. Slide frittata onto cutting board. Cut into wedges to serve.

EACH SERVING: ABOUT 215 CALORIES, 16G PROTEIN, 7G CARBOHYDRATE, 14G TOTAL FAT (4G SATURATED), 430MG CHOLESTEROL, 530MG SODIUM.

Eggs IN SPICY TOMATO SAUCE

This classic Italian dish pairs an easy homemade tomato sauce with eggs poached right in the sauce. It's a delicious one-skillet dish to add to your quick-cook repertoire.

ACTIVE TIME: 15 MINUTES   **TOTAL TIME:** 45 MINUTES   **MAKES:** 4 MAIN-DISH SERVINGS

1   loaf (8 ounces) Italian bread

1   tablespoon olive oil

1   jumbo onion (1 pound), cut into ¼-inch pieces

2   medium carrots, peeled and cut into ¼-inch pieces

1   stalk celery, cut into ¼-inch pieces

2   garlic cloves, crushed with garlic press

1   can (28 ounces) whole tomatoes

½   teaspoon salt

¼   teaspoon crushed red pepper

1   tablespoon butter or margarine

8   large eggs

¼   cup loosely packed fresh basil leaves, chopped

1   Preheat oven to 350°F. Cut bread diagonally into 1-inch-thick slices. Place bread slices on cookie sheet and bake until lightly toasted, about 5 minutes. Set aside.

2   In nonstick 12-inch skillet, heat oil over medium-high heat until hot. Add onion, carrots, celery, and garlic and cook, stirring occasionally, until vegetables are lightly browned, 12 to 15 minutes.

3   Stir in tomatoes with their juice, salt, and crushed red pepper, breaking up tomatoes with side of spoon; heat to boiling over medium-high heat. Reduce heat to low; simmer, stirring occasionally, 5 minutes. Stir in butter.

4   Break 1 egg into custard cup. With back of spoon, make small well in sauce and slip egg into well. Repeat with remaining eggs. Heat sauce to boiling over medium-high heat. Reduce heat to medium-low; cover and simmer until egg whites are set and yolks begin to thicken, 7 to 10 minutes, or until eggs are cooked to desired firmness.

5   To serve, place 1 bread slice in each of 4 large soup bowls. Spoon 2 eggs and some tomato mixture over each slice; sprinkle with basil. Serve with remaining bread.

....

EACH SERVING: ABOUT 455 CALORIES, 21G PROTEIN, 52G CARBOHYDRATE, 20G TOTAL FAT (6G SATURATED), 433MG CHOLESTEROL, 1,091MG SODIUM.

GROWN-UP **Pizza Bagel**

An updated version of your favorite "kiddy" snack.

ACTIVE TIME: 5 MINUTES   TOTAL TIME: 10 MINUTES   MAKES: 1 BAGEL

½ cup fresh mozzarella, cubed

1 bagel half, toasted

½ cup grape tomatoes, halved

1 tablespoon basil leaves, torn

1 teaspoon olive oil

⅛ teaspoon salt

1 Sprinkle cubed fresh mozzarella on 1 toasted bagel half; broil 1 to 2 minutes to melt slightly.

2 Top with ½ cup halved grape tomatoes, 1 tablespoon torn basil leaves, 1 teaspoon olive oil, and ⅛ teaspoon salt.

EACH SERVING: ABOUT 432 CALORIES, 19G PROTEIN, 38G CARBOHYDRATE, 22G TOTAL FAT (11G SATURATED), 58MG CHOLESTEROL, 686MG SODIUM.

Variations

CHOCOLATE-BANANA TREAT BAGEL

Spread **1 tablespoon chocolate-hazelnut spread** on **1 toasted bagel half**; top with **½ banana sliced**, and **2 tablespoon toasted sweetened shredded coconut**.

SWEET RICOTTA-STRAWBERRY BAGEL

Spread **¼ cup ricotta cheese** on **1 toasted bagel half**; top with **2 sliced strawberries** and **1 tablespoon balsamic vinegar** mixed with **½ teaspoon sugar**.

PROVENÇAL GOAT Cheese Tart

Doses of cream cheese and heavy cream are what make this goat cheese tart such a creamy treat. Top with tomatoes and chives to add a fresh touch to this rich dish. For photo, see page 50.

ACTIVE TIME: 25 MINUTES **TOTAL TIME:** 40 MINUTES **MAKES:** 4 MAIN-DISH SERVINGS

1 (9-inch) refrigerated ready-to-unroll pie crust

4 ounces goat cheese, softened

4 ounces reduced-fat cream cheese (Neufchâtel), softened

2 tablespoons heavy cream

2 tablespoons finely chopped fresh mint leaves

1 tablespoon snipped fresh chives, plus additional chives for garnish

⅛ teaspoon crumbled dried herbes de Provençe or thyme

⅛ teaspoon salt

⅛ teaspoon ground black pepper

2 (10 ounces each) heirloom tomatoes, preferably 1 green and 1 red, cored and cut crosswise into ¼-inch-thick slices

Cherry tomatoes, for garnish

1 Preheat oven to 450°F.

2 Gently press pie crust into 9-inch tart pan with removable bottom; prick all over with fork. Bake 14 minutes or until golden. Cool tart shell completely on wire rack.

3 Meanwhile, in medium bowl, whisk together goat cheese, cream cheese, and cream. Stir in mint, chives, herbes de Provençe, salt, and pepper.

4 Spread cheese mixture evenly in tart shell. Arrange tomatoes on top of filling, overlapping slices. Garnish with chives and cherry tomatoes. Tart can be assembled up to 1 hour before serving.

EACH SERVING: ABOUT 405 CALORIES, 11G PROTEIN, 30G CARBOHYDRATE, 29G TOTAL FAT (15G SATURATED), 50MG CHOLESTEROL, 545MG SODIUM.

GREENS AND RICOTTA **Pie**

It's like a quiche without the crust! Swiss chard and green onion make up this savory dish—an easy entrée for lunch or brunch.

ACTIVE TIME: 30 MINUTES   TOTAL TIME: 1 HOUR 10 MINUTES   MAKES: 6 MAIN-DISH SERVINGS

1   large head Swiss chard (about 1¾ pounds)

1   tablespoon olive oil

1   bunch green onions, cut into ¼-inch-thick pieces

½   teaspoon salt

¼   teaspoon ground black pepper

4   large eggs

1   container (15 ounces) part-skim ricotta cheese

¾   cup low-fat milk (1%)

½   cup freshly grated Parmesan cheese

2   tablespoons cornstarch

1   Preheat oven to 350°F. Grease 9½-inch deep-dish glass pie plate.

2   Trim off 2 inches from Swiss-chard stems; discard ends. Separate stems from leaves; thinly slice stems and coarsely chop leaves.

3   In nonstick 12-inch skillet, heat oil over medium-high heat until hot. Add sliced stems and cook, stirring frequently, until tender and lightly browned, about 4 minutes. Add green onions, salt, and pepper and cook 1 minute. Gradually add chopped leaves and cook, stirring, until leaves have wilted and excess moisture has evaporated, about 5 minutes.

4   In large bowl, with wire whisk, beat eggs, ricotta, milk, Parmesan, and cornstarch. Stir in Swiss-chard mixture.

5   Place prepared pie plate on foil-lined cookie sheet to catch any over-flow. Pour mixture into pie plate. Bake pie until knife inserted 2 inches from center comes out clean, about 40 minutes.

EACH SERVING: ABOUT 255 CALORIES, 19G PROTEIN, 14G CARBOHYDRATE, 14G TOTAL FAT (7G SATURATED), 172MG CHOLESTEROL, 680MG SODIUM.

TIP

The same amount of kale or collard greens can be substituted for the swiss chard, if desired.

ASPARAGUS **Omelet**

If you don't have pale yellow, nutty-flavored Gruyère cheese, substitute the same amount of shredded Swiss, some crumbled goat cheese, or a few shavings of fresh Parmesan.

ACTIVE TIME: 10 MINUTES   **TOTAL TIME:** 15 MINUTES   **MAKES:** 4 MAIN-DISH SERVINGS

FILLING

1   pound asparagus, trimmed

⅛   teaspoon ground black pepper

4   ounces Gruyère cheese, shredded (1 cup)

OMELETS

8   large eggs (see Tip below)

½   teaspoon salt

½   cup cold water

4   teaspoons butter or margarine

1 Prepare filling: In deep 12-inch skillet, heat 1 inch water to boiling over high heat. Add asparagus; heat to boiling. Reduce heat and simmer, uncovered, just until tender, about 5 minutes. Drain and rinse with cold running water. Drain. Sprinkle pepper over cheese.

2 Prepare omelets: In medium bowl, with wire whisk, beat eggs, salt, and cold water.

3 For each omelet, in nonstick 8-inch skillet, melt 1 teaspoon butter over medium-high heat. Pour in ½ cup egg mixture; cook, gently lifting edge of eggs with heat-safe rubber spatula and tilting pan to allow uncooked eggs to run underneath, until eggs are set, about 1 minute.

4 Sprinkle one-fourth of cheese mixture over half of omelet; top with one-fourth of asparagus spears. Fold unfilled half over filling and slide onto warm plate.

5 Repeat with remaining butter, egg mixture, and filling. If desired, keep omelets warm in 200°F oven until all are cooked.

EACH OMELET: ABOUT 310 CALORIES, 23G PROTEIN, 3G CARBOHYDRATE, 25G TOTAL FAT (11G SATURATED), 467MG CHOLESTEROL, 528MG SODIUM.

TIP

For lighter omelets, substitute 4 large eggs and 8 large egg whites for the whole eggs.

PTL SANDWICHES

This substantial fire-seared portobello burger, slathered with basil mayo and sandwiched in a ciabatta bun, is brawny enough for beef lovers. Before grilling, brush the mushrooms with rosemary-garlic oil for a robust flavor.

ACTIVE TIME: 20 MINUTES **TOTAL TIME:** 30 MINUTES **MAKES:** 4 SANDWICHES

- 1 teaspoon finely chopped fresh rosemary leaves
- 1 garlic clove, crushed with garlic press
- 3 tablespoons olive oil
- 3 tablespoons light mayonnaise
- 2 tablespoons packed, finely chopped fresh basil leaves
- 4 large portobello mushroom caps
- ¼ teaspoon salt
- ¼ teaspoon ground black pepper
- 4 ciabatta or other crusty rolls, split
- 4 iceberg lettuce leaves
- ½ cup arugula (optional)
- 1 ounce shaved Parmesan cheese
- 4 large tomato slices

1 Prepare outdoor grill for direct grilling on medium-high.

2 In small bowl, combine rosemary, garlic, and oil. In another bowl, combine mayonnaise and basil.

3 Brush oil mixture all over mushrooms, then sprinkle them with salt and pepper. Place ciabatta halves and mushrooms on hot grill grate. Cook ciabatta 3 minutes or until toasted, turning over once. Cook mushrooms 6 to 8 minutes or until browned and tender, turning over once. Transfer to cutting board. Cut mushrooms at an angle into ½-inch slices, keeping mushroom shape intact.

4 Spread basil mayonnaise on cut sides of ciabatta. Divide lettuce, then arugula (if using), among bottom halves. Place 1 mushroom on top, fanning slices apart slightly. Top with Parmesan, tomato, and ciabatta tops.

EACH SERVING: ABOUT 455 CALORIES, 15G PROTEIN, 61G CARBOHYDRATE, 18G TOTAL FAT (4G SATURATED), 14MG CHOLESTEROL, 845MG SODIUM.

TIP

To turn this recipe vegan, just use vegan mayonnaise and omit the cheese.

Old-Time Tomato SANDWICHES

The grated lemon peel and lemon juice perks up the mayo used in this tomato sandwich. We love these as is or with a few sprigs of basil or watercress tucked inside.

ACTIVE TIME: 15 MINUTES   TOTAL TIME: 15 MINUTES   MAKES: 4 SANDWICHES

1   lemon

⅓   cup mayonnaise

¼   teaspoon ground coriander

¼   teaspoon salt

¼   teaspoon ground black pepper

1   large round or oval loaf (1 pound) sourdough or other crusty bread

3   large ripe tomatoes, thickly sliced

1   From lemon, grate ½ teaspoon peel and squeeze 1 teaspoon juice. In small bowl, with fork, stir lemon peel and juice, mayonnaise, coriander, salt, and pepper until blended.

2   Cut eight ½-inch-thick slices from center of bread loaf. Reserve ends for another use. Toast bread if desired.

3   Spread 1 side of each bread slice with mayonnaise mixture. Top each of 4 bread slices, mayonnaise side up, with tomato slices; top with remaining bread slices, mayonnaise side down. Cut each sandwich in half to serve.

....

EACH SANDWICH: ABOUT 300 CALORIES, 6G PROTEIN, 35G CARBOHYDRATE, 18G TOTAL FAT (3G SATURATED), 7MG CHOLESTEROL, 540MG SODIUM.

VEGGIE FOCACCIA **Sandwiches**

Think of this as a Daywood, Italian-style: A slather of pesto plus marinated veggies between chewy bread. Cut in smaller squares and skewered, it works well as an appetizer, too.

ACTIVE TIME: 20 MINUTES   **TOTAL TIME:** 20 MINUTES   **YIELD:** 4 SANDWICHES

- 1 tablespoon red wine vinegar
- 1 tablespoon extra-virgin olive oil
- 1 small shallot, finely chopped
- ½ teaspoon chopped fresh thyme leaves
- ⅛ teaspoon salt
- ⅛ teaspoon ground black pepper
- 1 jar (9 to 10 ounces) artichoke hearts, rinsed, drained, and cut into quarters
- 1 jar (16 ounces) roasted red peppers, patted dry
- 3 ounces baby spinach leaves (5 cups)
- 4 pieces (5-inch-squares) focaccia bread
- ¼ cup prepared basil pesto
- 2 tablespoons mayonnaise
- 1 pound (1 large ball) fresh mozzarella cheese, thinly sliced

1 In small bowl, whisk together vinegar, oil, shallot, thyme, salt, and pepper. Place artichokes in a medium bowl, peppers in another bowl, and spinach in a third bowl. Divide dressing among all 3 bowls. Toss all food in bowls until well coated.

2 With serrated knife, split each focaccia square horizontally in half. In another small bowl, stir together pesto and mayonnaise. Spread on all cut sides of focaccia.

3 On each bottom half of focaccia, layer one-fourth each of spinach, peppers, mozzarella, and artichokes. Replace top halves of focaccia.

....

EACH SERVING: ABOUT 785 CALORIES, 31G PROTEIN, 69G CARBOHYDRATE, 43G TOTAL FAT (18G SATURATED), 97MG CHOLESTEROL, 1260MG SODIUM.

TIP

If your focaccia is more than 1½ inches high, you may want to cut a layer from the center to make the sandwich easier to eat.

VEGETARIAN **Souvlaki**

No one will miss the meat in these yummy sandwiches. Make the filling by cutting up your favorite veggie burgers.

ACTIVE TIME: 15 MINUTES   TOTAL TIME: 35 MINUTES   MAKES: 4 MAIN-DISH SERVINGS

1   tablespoon olive oil

1   large onion (12 ounces), cut in half and thinly sliced

4   frozen vegetarian soy burgers (10- to 12-ounce package), cut into 1- inch pieces

½   teaspoon salt

¼   teaspoon ground black pepper

8   ounces plain nonfat yogurt

8   ounces English (seedless) cucumber, cut into ¼-inch pieces

1   teaspoon dried mint

1   small garlic clove, crushed with garlic press

4   (6 to 7 inches) pitas, warmed

1   medium tomato, cut into ½-inch pieces

1   ounce feta cheese, crumbled

1 In nonstick 12-inch skillet, heat oil over medium heat until hot. Add onion and cook, stirring occasionally, until tender and golden, 12 to 15 minutes. Add burgers, ¼ teaspoon salt, and pepper and cook until heated through, about 5 minutes.

2 Meanwhile, in medium bowl, stir yogurt, cucumber, mint, garlic, and remaining ¼ teaspoon salt until blended. Add burger mixture and toss gently to combine.

3 Cut 1-inch slice from each pita to form pocket. Spoon one-fourth burger mixture into each pita. Sprinkle with tomato and feta.

EACH SANDWICH: ABOUT 390 CALORIES, 24G PROTEIN, 45G CARBOHYDRATE, 13G TOTAL FAT (3G SATURATED), 9MG CHOLESTEROL, 945MG SODIUM.

Falafel SANDWICHES

Serve these small, flat bean patties in pita pockets with lettuce, tomatoes, cucumbers, red onion, and tangy plain low-fat yogurt.

ACTIVE TIME: 10 MINUTES   TOTAL TIME: 26 MINUTES   MAKES: 4 SANDWICHES

4 green onions, cut into 1-inch pieces

2 garlic cloves, each cut in half

½ cup packed fresh flat-leaf parsley

2 teaspoons dried mint

1 can (15 to 19 ounces) garbanzo beans, rinsed and drained

½ cup plain dried bread crumbs

1 teaspoon ground coriander

1 teaspoon ground cumin

1 teaspoon baking powder

½ teaspoon salt

¼ teaspoon ground red pepper (cayenne)

¼ teaspoon ground allspice

olive oil cooking spray

4 (6- to 7-inch) pitas

accompaniments: sliced romaine lettuce, sliced tomatoes, sliced cucumber, sliced red onion, plain low-fat yogurt

1 In food processor, with knife blade attached, finely chop green onions, garlic, parsley, and mint. Add garbanzo beans, bread crumbs, coriander, cumin, baking powder, salt, ground red pepper, and allspice; blend until coarse puree forms.

2 Shape bean mixture, by scant ½ cups, into eight 3-inch round patties and place on sheet of waxed paper. Spray both sides of patties with olive oil spray.

3 Heat nonstick 10-inch skillet over medium-high heat until hot. Add half of patties and cook, turning once, until dark golden brown, about 8 minutes. Transfer the falafel patties to paper towels to drain. Repeat with remaining patties.

4 Cut off top third of each pita to form pocket. Place 2 warm patties in each pita. Serve with choice of accompaniments.

....

EACH SANDWICH WITHOUT ACCOMPANIMENTS: ABOUT 365 CALORIES, 14G PROTEIN, 68G CARBOHY-DRATE, 5G TOTAL FAT (1G SATURATED), 0MG CHOLES-TEROL, 1,015MG SODIUM.

Toasted Ravioli Salad
(page 73)

4 Main-Dish Salads

Salads can be an extremely versatile part of vegetarian menus year round. In this chapter you'll recognize variations on favorites, such as Egg Salad Deluxe, with sautéed onions and mushrooms.

Salads are an easy way to introduce international flair. There's Rice Noodles with Many Herbs, packed with fresh herbs and a drizzle of sesame oil, or Greek Peasant Salad, a feta-spiked glory. Italian-inspired salads include a Toasted Ravioli Salad, where ravioli is dipped in buttermilk and bread crumbs and baked until crispy and then tossed with arugula, roasted red peppers and a lemon-garlic dressing.

Salads are a great way to indulge your culinary creativity as you plan wholesome vegetarian meals for your family.

WHITE BEAN **Panzanella Salad**

Our version of Panzanella salad uses grilled bread, which adds a nice crunch and smoky flavor, plus a boost of protein from white kidney beans.

ACTIVE TIME: 25 MINUTES   **TOTAL TIME:** 30 MINUTES   **MAKES:** 6 SERVINGS

12 ounces Italian bread, cut into ¾ inch thick slices

6 tablespoons extra-virgin olive oil

2 tablespoons red wine vinegar

1 tablespoon drained and chopped capers

2 teaspoons Dijon mustard

¼ teaspoon dried oregano

³/₈ teaspoon salt

6³/₈ teaspoon ground black pepper

6 medium ripe tomatoes, chopped

12 ounces fresh mozzarella, cut in cubes

1 can (15 to 19 ounces) white kidney beans, rinsed and drained

1 bulb (large) fennel, cored, very thinly sliced, plus fronds for garnish

2 stalks celery, very thinly sliced

¼ cup fresh basil leaves, torn

1 Preheat outdoor grill for direct grilling on medium.

2 Brush bread slices with 2 tablespoons oil. Grill 5 to 6 minutes or until dark golden brown, turning over once. Cool slightly; cut into ¾-inch cubes.

3 In large bowl, whisk vinegar, capers, mustard, oregano, and ¼ teaspoon each salt and ground black pepper. Add remaining oil in slow, steady stream, whisking to blend.

4 To vinaigrette, add bread, tomatoes, mozzarella, beans, fennel, celery, basil, and ⅛ teaspoon each salt and pepper, tossing. Garnish with fennel fronds.

EACH SERVING: ABOUT 540 CALORIES, 20G PROTEIN, 50G CARBOHYDRATE, 29G TOTAL FAT (10G SATURATED), 45MG CHOLESTEROL, 760MG SODIUM.

TOMATO AND **Orzo Salad**

This perfect pasta toss requires little cooking but yields big flavor and will make you fall in love with the quick-cooking orzo if you haven't already.

ACTIVE TIME: 20 MINUTES   **TOTAL TIME:** 28 MINUTES   **MAKES:** 4 MAIN-DISH SERVINGS

1¼ cups orzo pasta

½ pound green beans, trimmed and each cut into thirds

2 large lemons

2 tablespoons extra-virgin olive oil

2 teaspoons fresh oregano leaves, chopped

¼ teaspoon ground black pepper

¾ teaspoon salt

1 pound ripe tomatoes (about 3 medium), cut into ½-inch pieces

4 ounces ricotta salata cheese, crumbled, or Parmesan cheese, shaved

1 In 4-quart saucepan, heat 3 quarts of *salted water* to boiling over high heat. Add orzo; heat to boiling and cook 4 minutes. Add green beans and cook until orzo and beans are tender, about 4 minutes longer. Drain well.

2 Meanwhile, from lemons, grate 1 teaspoon peel and squeeze ¼ cup juice. In large bowl, with wire whisk or fork, mix oil, oregano, salt, pepper, and lemon peel and juice until blended.

3 Add warm orzo and beans to dressing in bowl and toss well. Gently stir in tomatoes and ricotta salata.

....

EACH SERVING: ABOUT 340 CALORIES, 12G PROTEIN, 44G CARBOHYDRATE, 14G TOTAL FAT (6G SATURATED), 26MG CHOLESTEROL, 1,010MG SODIUM.

TIP

For a vegan Tomato and Orzo Salad recipe, just substitute soy cheese for the ricotta salata.

TOASTED **Ravioli Salad**

Only taking 20 minutes to make, this oven-toasted ravioli salad is a quick and decadent weeknight dinner solution. For photo, see page 68.

ACTIVE TIME: 7 MINUTES   TOTAL TIME: 20 MINUTES   MAKES: 4 SERVINGS

¾ cup dried bread crumbs

⅓ cup freshly grated Parmesan cheese

½ cup buttermilk

1 package (12-ounces) large cheese ravioli, fresh or frozen

olive oil cooking spray

2 tablespoons extra-virgin olive oil

1 lemon, juiced

1 garlic clove, crushed with garlic press

¼ teaspoon salt

¼ teaspoon ground black pepper

4 cups baby arugula

1 cup cherry tomatoes, halved

½ cup roasted red peppers, sliced

1 Preheat oven to 400°F. Whisk dried bread crumbs and grated Parmesan cheese in shallow bowl. Put buttermilk in another bowl.

2 Dip cheese ravioli in buttermilk, then crumb mixture, pressing gently to coat. Transfer to cookie sheet; spray generously with olive oil cooking spray. Bake 10 to 13 minutes or until crisp.

3 Meanwhile, in large bowl, whisk 2 tablespoons each extra-virgin olive oil and lemon juice; garlic, salt, and pepper. Add baby arugula, cherry tomatoes, and roasted red peppers; toss to combine.

4 Serve salad topped with ravioli, with shaved Parmesan cheese if desired.

EACH SERVING: ABOUT 455 CALORIES, 18G PROTEIN, 53G CARBOHYDRATE, 19G TOTAL FAT (8G SATURATED), 56MG CHOLESTEROL, 885MG SODIUM.

Rice Noodles WITH MANY HERBS

Whip up this light summer vegan main dish with fast-cooking noodles, carrots, cucumber, herbs, and our delicious Asian dressing. Serve warm or at room temperature, and pass the Sriracha sauce to add some treat.

ACTIVE TIME: 20 MINUTES   TOTAL TIME: 30 MINUTES   MAKES: 4 MAIN-DISH SERVINGS

3   small carrots, peeled and cut into 2" by ¼" matchstick strips (1 ⅓ cups)

⅓   cup seasoned rice vinegar

1   package (1 pound) ½-inch-wide flat rice noodles

⅓   English (seedless) cucumber, unpeeled and cut into 2" by ¼" matchstick strips (1 cup)

1   cup loosely packed fresh cilantro leaves

½   cup loosely packed fresh mint leaves

⅓   cup loosely packed small fresh basil leaves

⅓   cup snipped fresh chives

2   teaspoons Asian sesame oil

1 In small bowl, stir carrots with rice vinegar. Let stand at room temperature while preparing noodles.

2 In 8-quart saucepot, heat 5 quarts water to boiling over high heat. Add noodles and cook just until cooked through, about 3 minutes. Drain noodles; rinse under cold running water and drain again.

3 Transfer noodles to large shallow serving bowl. Add carrots with their liquid, cucumber, cilantro, mint, basil, chives, and sesame oil; toss well.

EACH SERVING: ABOUT 470 CALORIES, 7G PROTEIN, 105G CARBOHYDRATE, 3G TOTAL FAT (0G SATURATED), 0MG CHOLESTEROL, 550MG SODIUM.

TIP
These thin, translucent white noodles are made from rice flour and water; their neutral flavor makes them a perfect foil for robust flavors.

GREEK **Peasant Salad**

Serve this cool Mediterranean-style salad on a summer night with a side of crusty rolls—the better to dip into the salad's vinaigrette.

ACTIVE TIME: 25 MINUTES   TOTAL TIME: 25 MINUTES   MAKES: 4 MAIN-DISH SERVINGS

4   Kirby cucumbers (about 1 pound)

2   tablespoons fresh lemon juice

1   tablespoon olive oil

¼   teaspoon salt

⅛   teaspoon ground black pepper

2   pounds ripe red and/or yellow tomatoes (about 6 medium), cut into 1-inch pieces

½   cup loosely packed fresh mint leaves, chopped

⅓   cup Kalamata olives, pitted and coarsely chopped

¼   cup loosely packed fresh dill, chopped

2   ounces feta cheese, crumbled (½ cup)

1 With vegetable peeler, remove 3 or 4 evenly spaced lengthwise strips of peel from each cucumber. Cut each cucumber lengthwise into quarters, then crosswise into ½-inch pieces.

2 In large bowl, with wire whisk or fork, mix lemon juice, oil, salt, and pepper until blended. Add cucumbers, tomatoes, mint, olives, and dill, and toss until evenly mixed and coated with dressing. Top with feta.

....

EACH SERVING: ABOUT 150 CALORIES, 5G PROTEIN, 17G CARBOHYDRATE, 9G TOTAL FAT (3G SATURATED), 12MG CHOLESTEROL, 42G SODIUM.

Couscous WITH GARBANZO BEANS

A vegetarian entrée fragrant with the flavors of Morocco—warm spices, green olives, and garlic—gets a quick start from pre-seasoned couscous mix.

ACTIVE TIME: 5 MINUTES   **TOTAL TIME:** 15 MINUTES   **MAKES:** 4 MAIN-DISH SERVINGS

1   box (5.6 ounces) couscous (Moroccan pasta) with toasted pine nuts

⅓   cup dark seedless raisins

1   tablespoon olive oil

1   medium zucchini (about 10 ounces), cut lengthwise in half, then crosswise into ½-inch-thick slices

1   garlic clove, crushed with garlic press

¾   teaspoon ground cumin

¾   teaspoon ground coriander

⅛   teaspoon ground red pepper (cayenne)

2   cans (15 to 19 ounces each) garbanzo beans, rinsed and drained

½   cup salad olives, drained, or chopped pimiento-stuffed olives

¼   cup water

1   Prepare couscous as label directs, except add raisins to cooking water.

2   Meanwhile, in nonstick 12-inch skillet, heat oil over medium-high heat until hot. Add zucchini and cook, stirring occasionally, 5 minutes. Add garlic, cumin, coriander, and red pepper and cook, stirring, 30 seconds. Add beans, olives, and water and cook, stirring often, until heated through, about 5 minutes.

3   Add cooked couscous to bean mixture and toss gently. Spoon into serving bowl.

....

EACH SERVING: ABOUT 555 CALORIES, 20G PROTEIN, 101G CARBOHYDRATE, 10G TOTAL FAT (1G SATURATED), 0MG CHOLESTEROL, 1,110MG SODIUM.

WARM FRENCH **Lentil Salad**

A classic French dish, warm lentil salad is at once healthful, hearty, and comforting. The bell peppers offer a good source of vitamin C and anti-oxidants.

ACTIVE TIME: 20 MINUTES   **TOTAL TIME:** 50 MINUTES   **MAKES:** 4 SERVINGS

7   ounces French green (de Puy) lentils (1 cup), picked over and rinsed

3   sprigs fresh oregano

¼   teaspoon oregano leaves, chopped

1   medium (8 ounces) onion

3   large stalks celery

2   large peppers (red, orange, or yellow)

2   tablespoons extra-virgin olive oil

½   teaspoon salt

½   teaspoon ground black pepper

3   tablespoons red wine vinegar

1   tablespoon fresh dill, chopped, plus more for garnish

6   ounces baby spinach

2   ounces feta cheese, crumbled (½ cup)

1   In 4-quart saucepan, combine lentils, oregano sprigs, and *3 cups wate*r. Cover; heat to boiling. Reduce heat to maintain simmer; cook 25 to 30 minutes or until tender.

2   Meanwhile, chop onion, celery, and peppers. In 12-inch skillet, heat 1 tablespoon oil on medium. Add onion and celery; cook 7 to 8 minutes or until tender, stirring. Add peppers, *2 tablespoons water*, and ¼ teaspoon each salt and pepper. Cook 5 minutes or until peppers are crisp-tender, stirring.

3   Drain lentils (discard sprigs); transfer to bowl. Stir in vinegar, dill, oregano leaves, onion mixture, ¼ teaspoon each salt and pepper, and remaining oil.

4   Divide spinach among 4 serving plates; spoon lentil mixture over. Top with feta, and garnish with dill.

EACH SERVING: ABOUT 340 CALORIES, 16G PROTEIN, 47G CARBOHYDRATE, 12G TOTAL FAT (3G SATURATED), 13MG CHOLESTEROL, 565MG SODIUM.

Egg Salad DELUXE

Hard-cooked eggs are chopped and mixed with sautéed onions, mushrooms, and celery for a new take on the classic egg salad. If you like, serve with toasted whole-grain bread.

ACTIVE TIME: 20 MINUTES   TOTAL TIME: 40 MINUTES   MAKES: 6 MAIN-DISH SERVINGS

8 large eggs

3 tablespoons olive oil

1 medium onion, cut in half and thinly sliced

10 ounces mushrooms, sliced

2 medium stalks celery, finely chopped

¼ cup loosely packed fresh parsley leaves, chopped

½ teaspoon salt

¼ teaspoon ground black pepper

1 head Boston lettuce, leaves separated

1 In 3-quart saucepan, place eggs and enough cold water to cover by at least 1 inch; heat to boiling over high heat. Immediately remove saucepan from heat and cover tightly; let stand 15 minutes. Pour off hot water and run cold water over eggs until easy to handle.

2 Meanwhile, in nonstick 12-inch skillet, heat 1 tablespoon oil over medium heat until hot. Add onion and cook, stirring occasionally, until tender and golden, 10 to 12 minutes. Increase heat to medium-high; add mushrooms and cook until mushrooms are golden and all liquid has evaporated, about 8 minutes.

3 Peel hard-cooked eggs and finely chop. In large bowl, combine eggs with mushroom mixture, celery, parsley, salt, pepper, and remaining 2 tablespoons oil; toss well.

4 To serve, line platter with lettuce leaves and top with egg salad.

EACH SERVING: ABOUT 190 CALORIES, 11G PROTEIN, 5G CARBOHYDRATE, 14G TOTAL FAT (3G SATURATED), 283MG CHOLESTEROL, 290MG SODIUM.

CHICKPEA MANGO **Salad**

This aromatic salad borrows flavors from Indian cuisine and is packed with vitamins and antioxidants, thanks to a combination of chickpeas, mango, baby spinach, and almonds.

ACTIVE TIME: 20 MINUTES   TOTAL TIME: 20 MINUTES   MAKES: 4 MAIN-DISH SERVINGS

½ cup plain fat-free yogurt

½ cup loosely packed fresh cilantro leaves

2 tablespoons mango chutney

1 tablespoon extra-virgin olive oil

2 teaspoons fresh lime juice

½ teaspoon ground coriander

½ teaspoon salt

¼ teaspoon pepper

2 cans (15 ounces each) no-salt-added garbanzo beans (chickpeas), drained

1 large ripe mango, chopped

1 package (5- to 6-ounce) baby spinach

½ cup sliced almonds, toasted

naan (Indian-style flatbread) or pita bread, toasted, for serving

1 In food processor, puree yogurt, cilantro, chutney, oil, lime juice, coriander, salt, and pepper until smooth. Transfer to large bowl.

2 To same bowl, add beans and mango. Toss until well-coated. Chickpea mixture can be made ahead and refrigerated in airtight container up to overnight. To serve, add spinach and almonds; toss to combine. Serve with naan.

EACH SERVING: ABOUT 435 CALORIES, 18G PROTEIN, 69G CARBOHYDRATE, 11G TOTAL FAT (1G SATURATED), 1MG CHOLESTEROL, 560MG SODIUM.

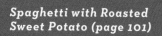
Spaghetti with Roasted Sweet Potato (page 101)

5 Quick Dinners

We all live hectic lives today. So we've put together a collection of scrumptious recipes that require the bare minimum of muss, fuss, labor.

Eggs are the basis of an airy spinach soufflé and several savory frittatas; black beans take center stage stuffed into sweet potatoes and layered in a Tex-Mex Tortilla Pizza; vegetables abound in Fast Fried Rice. Pizza dough comes to the rescue to make a quick Ricotta-Spinach Calzone and phyllo dough serves as the base for Vegetable Phyllo Pizza. Or, go Italian with a twist on the classic in Broccoli Pesto Spaghetti or the Marsala-spiked Fettuccini with Mushrooms and Cream.

Another great feature of the time-saving nature of these dishes is that few pots and pans are used in preparation. That means cleanup is a breeze, allowing you to spend more time with your family.

RICOTTA-SPINACH **Calzone**

Using refrigerated pizza-crust dough simplifies and shortens the preparation of these rich cheese and spinach-filled "pies." Any extra marinara sauce can be used to dip the calzone into.

ACTIVE TIME: 10 MINUTES   **TOTAL TIME:** 35 MINUTES   **MAKES:** 4 MAIN-DISH SERVINGS

1   cup part-skim ricotta cheese

1   cup shredded mozzarella cheese (4 ounces)

1   tablespoon cornstarch

½   teaspoon dried oregano

1   tube (10 ounces) refrigerated pizza-crust dough

½   cup marinara sauce

1   package (10 ounces) frozen chopped spinach, thawed and squeezed dry

1   Preheat oven to 400°F. In small bowl, combine ricotta, mozzarella, cornstarch, and oregano; stir until blended. Set aside.

2   Spray large cookie sheet with nonstick cooking spray. Unroll pizza dough in center of cookie sheet. With fingertips, press dough into 14" by 10" rectangle.

3   Spread cheese mixture lengthwise on half of dough, leaving 1-inch border. Spoon marinara sauce over cheese mixture; top with spinach. Fold other half of dough over filling. Pinch edges together to seal.

4   Bake calzone until well browned on top, 20 to 25 minutes. Cut calzone into 4 equal pieces to serve.

EACH SERVING: ABOUT 400 CALORIES, 21G PROTEIN, 43G CARBOHYDRATE, 15G TOTAL FAT (5G SATURATED), 19MG CHOLESTEROL, 1,055MG SODIUM

BROCCOLI PESTO **Spaghetti**

The pesto is best made in a food processor; a blender makes the mixture too creamy. Serve with breadsticks and a green salad splashed with balsamic vinegar.

ACTIVE TIME: 8 MINUTES   TOTAL TIME: 20 MINUTES   MAKES: 4 MAIN-DISH SERVINGS

1 package (16 ounces) spaghetti or thin spaghetti

1 bag (16 ounces) frozen chopped broccoli

1 cup vegetable broth

¼ cup freshly grated Parmesan cheese

2 tablespoons olive oil

1 small garlic clove

¼ teaspoon salt

ground black pepper

1 In large saucepot, cook pasta as label directs. In saucepan, prepare broccoli as label directs.

2 In food processor, with knife blade attached, puree cooked broccoli, broth, Parmesan, oil, garlic, and salt until smooth, stopping processor occasionally to scrape down side.

3 Drain pasta; transfer to warm serving bowl. Add broccoli pesto to pasta; toss well. Sprinkle with pepper and serve.

EACH SERVING: ABOUT 550 CALORIES, 22G PROTEIN, 91G CARBOHYDRATE, 11G TOTAL FAT (3G SATURATED), 5MG CHOLESTEROL, 615MG SODIUM.

VEGETARIAN PHYLLO **Pizza**

Delicate layers of phyllo form the crispy, flaky crust of this rich, savory pizza that holds goat cheese-smothered artichoke hearts and grape tomatoes.

ACTIVE TIME: 10 MINUTES   TOTAL TIME: 25 MINUTES   MAKES: 4 MAIN-DISH SERVINGS

6   sheets (17" by 12" each) fresh or frozen (thawed) phyllo

2   tablespoons butter or margarine, melted

4   ounces soft, mild goat cheese, such as Montrâchet

1   jar (6 ounces) marinated artichoke hearts, drained and cut into ¼-inch pieces

1½ cups grape or cherry tomatoes, each cut in half

1   Preheat oven to 450°F. Place 1 sheet of phyllo on ungreased large cookie sheet; brush with some melted butter. Repeat layering with remaining phyllo and butter. Do not brush top layer.

2   Crumble goat cheese over phyllo; top with artichokes and tomatoes. Bake pizza until golden brown around the edges, 12 to 15 minutes.

3   Transfer pizza to large cutting board. With pizza cutter or knife, cut pizza lengthwise in half, then cut each half crosswise into 4 pieces.

EACH SERVING: ABOUT 245 CALORIES, 8G PROTEIN, 20G CARBOHYDRATE, 19G TOTAL FAT(9G SATURATED), 29MG CHOLESTEROL, 387MG SODIUM.

TEX-MEX **Tortilla Pizza**

Entice your palate with this colorful and tasty Tex-Mex-inspired pizza made from layers of flour tortillas topped with zesty pepper jack cheese, salsa, beans, and avocado.

ACTIVE TIME: 13 MINUTES   **TOTAL TIME:** 25 MINUTES   **MAKES:** 4 MAIN-DISH SERVINGS

4   (8-inch) flour tortillas

1   can (15 ounces) fat-free refried beans

½   teaspoon chili powder

¼   teaspoon ground cumin

1   can (15 to 19 ounces) no-salt-added kidney beans, rinsed

1   cup shredded pepper jack cheese

1   avocado, peeled, pitted, and sliced

1   cup chunky salsa

3   cups shredded romaine lettuce

Lime wedges, for serving

1 Arrange oven racks in top and bottom thirds of oven. Preheat oven to 475°F. Spray 2 large cookie sheets with nonstick cooking spray; place 2 tortillas on each.

2 Combine refried beans, chili powder, and ground cumin; spread on tortillas. Top with kidney beans, shredded pepper jack cheese, and avocado slices.

3 Bake 12 minutes or until tortillas are crisp around edges, switching racks halfway through cooking. Top with chunky salsa and shredded romaine lettuce. Serve with limes.

EACH SERVING: ABOUT 650 CALORIES, 29G PROTEIN, 67G CARBOHYDRATE, 29G TOTAL FAT (13G SATURATED), 67MG CHOLESTEROL, 1,485MG SODIUM.

SKILLET VEGETABLE **Curry**

As the vegetables simmer, toast some naan or pita bread. A sprinkle of flaked coconut and mustard seeds add South Indian flair to the vegan-friendly dish.

ACTIVE TIME: 15 MINUTES   **TOTAL TIME:** 35 MINUTES   **MAKES:** 4 MAIN-DISH SERVINGS

¾   pound cauliflower flowerets

1   large all-purpose potato (about 8 ounces), peeled and cut into 1-inch pieces

1   large sweet potato (about 12 ounces), peeled and cut into 1-inch pieces

2   tablespoons lightly packed sweetened flaked coconut

2   teaspoons olive oil

1   medium onion (8 ounces) finely chopped

1   teaspoon mustard seeds

1½ teaspoons ground cumin

1½ teaspoons ground coriander

⅛   teaspoon ground red pepper (cayenne)

2   medium tomatoes, chopped

1   cup frozen peas, thawed

1¼ teaspoons salt

½   cup loosely packed fresh cilantro leaves, chopped

1 In 4-quart saucepan, combine cauliflower, potato, sweet potato, and enough water to cover; heat to boiling over high heat. Reduce heat to low; cover and simmer until vegetables are tender, 8 to 10 minutes. Drain well, reserving ¾ cup cooking water.

2 Meanwhile, in dry nonstick 12-inch skillet, cook coconut over medium heat, stirring constantly, until lightly browned, about 3 minutes; transfer to small bowl.

3 In same skillet, heat oil over medium heat until hot; add onion and cook 5 minutes. Add mustard seeds, cumin, coriander, and ground red pepper; cover and cook, shaking skillet frequently, until onion is tender and lightly browned and seeds start to pop, 5 minutes longer.

4 Spoon cauliflower mixture into skillet. Add tomatoes, peas, salt, and reserved cooking water; heat through. Sprinkle with cilantro to serve.

ACH SERVING: ABOUT 230 CALORIES, 8G PROTEIN, G CARBOHYDRATE, 4G TOTAL FAT (1G SATURATED), 0 CHOLESTEROL, 735MG SODIUM.

FAST **Fried Rice**

The secrets to this dish are quick-cooking brown rice, pre-cut frozen vegetables, and ready-to-use stir-fry sauce.

ACTIVE TIME: 5 MINUTES   **TOTAL TIME:** 20 MINUTES   **MAKES:** 4 MAIN-DISH SERVINGS

1½ cups quick-cooking brown rice

1   pound firm tofu, drained and cut into 1-inch cubes

6   teaspoons olive oil

1   package (16 ounces) frozen vegetables for stir-fry

2   large eggs, lightly beaten

⅓   cup stir-fry sauce

¼   cup water

1 Prepare rice as label directs.

2 Meanwhile, in medium bowl, place 3 layers paper towels. Place tofu on towels and top with 3 more layers of paper towels. With hand, gently press tofu to extract excess moisture.

3 In nonstick 12-inch skillet, heat 2 teaspoons oil over medium-high heat until hot. Add frozen vegetables; cover and cook, stirring occasionally, 5 minutes. Transfer vegetables to bowl; keep warm.

4 In same skillet, heat remaining 4 teaspoons oil until hot. Add tofu and cook, stirring gently, 5 minutes. Stir in cooked rice and cook 4 minutes longer.

5 With spatula, push rice mixture around edge of skillet, leaving space in center. Add eggs to center of skillet; cook, stirring eggs until scrambled, about 1 minute. Add stir-fry sauce, vegetables, and water; cook, stirring, 1 minute.

....

EACH SERVING: ABOUT 360 CALORIES, 17G PROTEIN, 41G CARBOHYDRATE, 15G TOTAL FAT (2G SATURATED), 106MG CHOLESTEROL, 760MG SODIUM.

TIP

If you have more time, chop a combo of carrots, broccoli, onion, and celery so you have a total of 3 to 4 cups and cook as in step 3.

BEAN AND CORN-STUFFED
Sweet Potatoes

This dish is the perfect, easy weeknight dinner for the whole family. Packed with healthy veggies like spinach and fiber-loaded beans, this is a great alternative to a boring baked potato.

ACTIVE TIME: 10 MINUTES **TOTAL TIME:** 20 MINUTES **MAKES:** 4 SERVINGS

4 sweet potatoes, pricked with fork

1 tablespoon olive oil

1 medium onion, sliced

1 can (15-ounces) black beans, rinsed and drained

2 cups packed baby spinach

1 cup corn

½ cup sliced green onions

1 tablespoon chopped chipotle chiles in adobo

1 garlic clove, crushed with garlic press

¼ teaspoon salt

4 tablespoons shredded low-fat Mexican-blend cheese

1 Microwave sweet potatoes, pricked with fork, on high for 10 minutes or until tender, turning over once.

2 Meanwhile, heat olive oil in 12-inch skillet on medium-high heat. Add sliced onion and cook 6 to 7 minutes or until soft, stirring frequently.

3 Add black beans, baby spinach, corn, sliced green onion, chopped chipotle chiles in adobo, garlic, and salt. Cook 2 minutes or until spinach wilts.

4 Split sweet potatoes and fill with bean mixture. Sprinkle each with 1 tablespoon shredded low-fat Mexican-blend cheese.

EACH SERVING: ABOUT 265 CALORIES, 10G PROTEIN, 50G CARBOHYDRATE, 5G TOTAL FAT (2G SATURATED), 4MG CHOLESTEROL, 555MG SODIUM.

TIP

For a vegan recipe, just substitute soy cheese for the Mexican-blend cheese or omit it altogether.

Fettuccine WITH MUSHROOMS AND CREAM

Don't go out for pasta when you can whip up a hearty dish in your own kitchen. Sun-dried tomatoes and Marsala wine perk up this fettuccine and mushroom toss.

ACTIVE TIME: 15 MINUTES   **TOTAL TIME:** 33 MINUTES   **MAKES:** 4 MAIN-DISH SERVINGS

2   packages (9 ounces each) refrigerated fettuccine pasta

1   tablespoon olive oil

1   small shallot, finely chopped (2 tablespoons)

8   ounces shiitake mushrooms, stems removed, and caps thinly sliced

8   ounces white mushrooms, trimmed and thinly sliced

½   teaspoon salt

¼   cup Marsala wine

1½ cups vegetable broth

⅓   cup heavy or whipping cream

1   cup loosely packed fresh basil or parsley leaves, chopped

¼   cup sun-dried tomatoes in olive oil, sliced

1   In large saucepot, cook pasta as label directs.

2   Meanwhile, in nonstick 12-inch skillet, heat oil over medium-high heat until hot. Add shallot and cook, stirring occasionally, 1 minute. Add mushrooms and salt and cook, stirring occasionally, until tender and golden, 10 to 12 minutes.

3   Stir in the wine. Heat to boiling over medium-high heat and cook 1 minute. Add the broth and cream; heat to boiling and cook, stirring, 3 minutes.

4   Drain fettuccine and return to saucepot. Add mushroom mixture, basil, and sun-dried tomatoes and cook over medium heat, tossing until evenly coated, 1 minute.

....

EACH SERVING: ABOUT 560 CALORIES, 20G PROTEIN, 83G CARBOHYDRATE, 18G TOTAL FAT (7G SATURATED), 158MG CHOLESTEROL, 815MG SODIUM.

MEXICAN POTATO **Frittata**

This flat, baked omelet combines a jar of salsa with a bit of sharp Cheddar cheese. Toss a package of prewashed baby spinach with sliced red onions, sliced fresh pears, and bottled salad dressing while the frittata bakes.

ACTIVE TIME: 20 MINUTES   **TOTAL TIME:** 25 MINUTES   **MAKES:** 4 MAIN-DISH SERVINGS

1   teaspoon olive oil

12   ounces red-skinned potatoes, cut into ½-inch pieces

6   large eggs

1   jar (11 to 12 ounces) medium-hot salsa

½   teaspoon salt

¼   teaspoon ground black pepper

¼   cup shredded sharp Cheddar cheese (1 ounce)

1   medium tomato

1   Preheat oven to 425°F. In oven-safe nonstick 10-inch skillet (if skillet is not oven-safe, wrap handle with double layer of foil), heat oil over medium-high heat until hot; add potatoes and cook, covered, until potatoes are tender and golden brown, about 10 minutes, stirring occasionally.

2   Meanwhile, in medium bowl, with wire whisk or fork, beat eggs with ¼ cup salsa (chopped, if necessary), salt, and pepper. Stir in cheese; set aside. Chop tomato and stir into remaining salsa.

3   Stir egg mixture into potatoes in skillet and cook over medium heat, covered, until egg mixture begins to set around edge, about 3 minutes. Remove lid and place skillet in oven; bake until frittata is set, 4 to 6 minutes.

4   To serve, transfer frittata to cutting board. Cut into wedges and top with salsa mixture.

EACH SERVING: ABOUT 235 CALORIES, 14G PROTEIN, 20G CARBOHYDRATE, 11G TOTAL FAT (4G SATURATED), 327MG CHOLESTEROL, 795MG SODIUM.

Spaghetti WITH ROASTED SWEET POTATO

This simple pasta is perfect for weeknight cooking, and loaded with healthy, vitamin A-rich sweet potatoes. For photo, see page 86.

ACTIVE TIME: 10 MINUTES   TOTAL TIME: 35 MINUTES   MAKES: 4 SERVINGS

2 sweet potatoes, cubed

3 tablespoons olive oil

3 sprigs fresh rosemary

3/4 teaspoon salt

12 ounces spaghetti

1/3 cup pine nuts

2/3 cup finely grated Parmesan cheese

1 Preheat oven to 475°F. On parchment paper–lined jelly-roll pan, toss cubed sweet potatoes, 1 tablespoon olive oil, rosemary, and ½ teaspoon salt. Roast 15 minutes or until tender.

2 Meanwhile, heat large covered saucepot of *salted water* to boiling on high. Add spaghetti; cook as label directs.

3 Place pine nuts in medium bowl. Microwave on high 1 to 2 minutes or until lightly toasted.

4 Drain pasta, reserving *¼ cup cooking water*. In large bowl, toss pasta, sweet potatoes, pine nuts, Parmesan cheese, remaining 2 tablespoons olive oil, remaining ¼ teaspoon salt, and the reserved cooking water.

EACH SERVING: ABOUT 605 CALORIES, 20G PROTEIN, 80G CARBOHYDRATE, 24G TOTAL FAT (5G SATURATED), 12MG CHOLESTEROL, 780MG SODIUM.

TIP

Omit the parmesan cheese in this pasta (or substitute with nutritional yeast) to turn vegan.

SPINACH **Soufflé**

Even though this recipe requires about 40 minutes total, only 20 minutes are active prep. During the remaining 20 minutes, while the soufflé bakes, you can relax! Serve with crusty rolls and a salad of mixed baby greens.

ACTIVE TIME: 20 MINUTES   **TOTAL TIME:** 40 MINUTES   **MAKES:** 4 MAIN-DISH SERVINGS

3   tablespoons plain dried bread crumbs

1½ cups low-fat milk (1%)

⅓   cup cornstarch

2   large eggs, separated

1   package (10 ounces) frozen chopped spinach, thawed and squeezed dry

3   tablespoons freshly grated Parmesan cheese

½   teaspoon salt

¼   teaspoon ground black pepper

½   teaspoon cream of tartar

4   large egg whites

1 Preheat oven to 425°F. Spray 10-inch quiche dish or shallow 2-quart casserole with nonstick cooking spray; sprinkle with bread crumbs to coat. Set aside.

2 In 2-quart saucepan, with wire whisk, beat milk with cornstarch until blended. Heat milk mixture over medium-high heat, stirring constantly, until mixture thickens and boils; boil 1 minute. Remove pan from heat.

3 In large bowl, with rubber spatula, mix egg yolks, spinach, Parmesan, salt, and pepper until blended; stir in warm milk mixture. Cool slightly (if spinach mixture is too warm, it will deflate beaten egg whites).

4 In another large bowl, with mixer at high speed, beat cream of tartar and 6 egg whites until stiff peaks form. Gently fold egg-white mixture, one-third at a time, into spinach mixture.

5 Spoon soufflé mixture into quiche dish. Bake soufflé until top is golden and puffed, about 20 minutes. Serve immediately.

EACH SERVING: ABOUT 195 CALORIES, 15G PROTEIN, 23G CARBOHYDRATE, 5G TOTAL FAT (2G SATURATED), 114MG CHOLESTEROL, 590MG SODIUM.

RAVIOLI-GREEN BEAN **Lasagna**

Fast and easy, cheesy lasagna in only 35 minutes. The trick is pre-made fresh or frozen ravioli for a great weeknight meal. Green beans in the mix give an added veggie boost.

ACTIVE TIME: 10 MINUTES   **TOTAL TIME:** 35 MINUTES   **MAKES:** 6 SERVINGS

½   pound thin green beans

3   tablespoons water

1   cup part-skim ricotta cheese

1   cup shredded Provolone cheese

½   cup freshly grated Parmesan cheese

1½ cups prepared marinara sauce

2   packages (12-ounces) large cheese ravioli, fresh or frozen

1   Preheat oven to 375°F. In large bowl, place thin green beans and water; cover and microwave on High 3 minutes or until tender.

2   Meanwhile, in medium bowl, mix part-skim ricotta cheese, ½ cup shredded provolone cheese, and ¼ cup grated Parmesan cheese.

3   Spread, in 2-quart baking dish, ¾ cup prepared marinara sauce. Top with 1 package cheese ravioli, ricotta mixture, and green beans. Top with another package cheese ravioli and the remaining marinara sauce.

4   Sprinkle with the remaining provolone cheese and grated Parmesan cheese; bake 25 minutes or until bubbling and golden brown.

EACH SERVING: ABOUT 540 CALORIES, 29G PROTEIN, 58G CARBOHYDRATE, 21G TOTAL FAT (12G SATURATED), 99MG CHOLESTEROL, 1,240MG SODIUM.

QUICK DINNERS

Grilled Tomato and Basil Pizzas (page 114)

6 One-Dish Meals

Is there a cook anywhere without a favorite one-dish meal in her or his repertoire? Maybe it's a comforting casserole you turn to when you're entertaining or an easy stir-fry on PTA night.

Gather the family for a cozy dinner of Lasagna Toss with Spinach and Ricotta or dive into Cauliflower Mac and Cheese. Having friends over for a casual dinner and game night? Tomato and Cheese Pie, a fluffy custard of tomatoes, ricotta, and basil. For an easy al fresco summer meal, fire up the coals for Grilled Tomato and Basil Pizzas. And when the leaves begin to fall, Moroccan-Spiced Sweet Potato Medley will satisfy the need for stick-to-the-ribs comfort food.

As you work your way through these delectable recipes, don't be surprised to find that your repertoire of favorite one-dish meals has grown to include many of those on these pages.

Lasagna Toss WITH SPINACH AND RICOTTA

This recipe has all the flavor of a layered and baked lasagna, without the wait! Lasagna noodles are tossed with a speedy tomato-spinach skillet sauce, then dolloped with ricotta cheese to serve. Use tofu ricotta to make this recipe vegan.

ACTIVE TIME: 20 MINUTES   **TOTAL TIME:** 55 MINUTES   **MAKES:** 4 MAIN-DISH SERVINGS

1   package (16 ounces) lasagna noodles

1   tablespoon olive oil

1   medium onion, finely chopped

2   garlic cloves, crushed with garlic press

1   can (28 ounces) plum tomatoes

¾   teaspoon salt

¼   teaspoon ground black pepper

1   package (10 ounces) frozen chopped spinach

½   cup loosely packed fresh basil leaves, chopped

¼   cup freshly grated Parmesan cheese, plus additional for serving (optional)

1   cup part-skim ricotta cheese

1   In large saucepot, cook lasagna noodles as label directs, increasing cooking time to 12 to 14 minutes.

2   Meanwhile, in nonstick 12-inch skillet, heat oil over medium heat until hot. Add onion and cook, stirring occasionally, until tender, about 10 minutes. Add garlic and cook, stirring, 30 seconds.

3   Stir in tomatoes with their juice, salt, and pepper, breaking up tomatoes with side of spoon; heat to boiling over high heat. Reduce heat to medium and cook, uncovered, 8 minutes. Add frozen spinach and cook, covered, until spinach is tender, about 10 minutes, stirring occasionally. Stir in basil.

4   Drain noodles; return to saucepot. Add tomato mixture and Parmesan; toss well. Spoon into 4 pasta bowls; top with dollops of ricotta cheese. Serve with additional Parmesan, if you like.

EACH SERVING: ABOUT 620 CALORIES, 28G PROTEIN, 100G CARBOHYDRATE, 12G TOTAL FAT (5G SATURATED), 23MG CHOLESTEROL, 1,640MG SODIUM.

TIP

Tempted to cook up no-boil lasagna noodles to save time? Don't: They'll break apart when tossed.

TEX-MEX **Lasagna**

Beans, corn, chili powder, and salsa recreate this classic, gooey dish with southwestern flair. No-boil lasagna noodles mean you spend less time making and more time savoring your dinner.

ACTIVE TIME: 20 MINUTES **TOTAL TIME:** 1 HOUR 15 MINUTES **MAKES:** 6 SERVINGS

2 teaspoons vegetable oil

1 small (4 to 6 ounce) onion, chopped

2 medium zucchini, thinly sliced

1 jar (16 ounces) salsa

1 cup corn, fresh or frozen (thawed)

1 tablespoon no-salt-added chili powder

1 can (8-ounce) tomato sauce

6 oven-ready (no-boil) lasagna noodles

1 can fat-free refried beans

8 ounce shredded Monterey Jack or Cheddar cheese

½ cup packed fresh cilantro leaves

1 Preheat oven to 400°F. Spray shallow 2-quart baking dish with nonstick cooking spray.

2 In 12-inch skillet, heat oil on medium. Add onion. Cook 2 minutes or until beginning to soften, stirring occasionally. Stir in zucchini, salsa, corn, and chili powder. Cook 2 to 3 minutes or until zucchini is crisp-tender, stirring occasionally. Remove from heat.

3 On bottom of prepared dish, spread half of tomato sauce. Arrange 2 lasagna noodles in single layer. Top with half of beans and half of vegetables. Arrange 2 more lasagna noodles in single layer. Top with half of cheese. Repeat with remaining sauce, noodles, beans, and vegetables. Top with remaining cheese.

4 Cover tightly with foil and bake 30 minutes. Remove foil and bake another 15 to 20 minutes or until bubbly and noodles are tender. Remove from oven; let stand 5 minutes. Top with cilantro.

EACH SERVING: ABOUT 365 CALORIES, 18G PROTEIN, 41G CARBOHYDRATE, 15G TOTAL FAT (8G SATURATED), 34MG CHOLESTEROL, 960MG SODIUM.

SPINACH AND ARTICHOKE **Pizza**

This creamy French bread pizza with fresh spinach, cream cheese, and artichoke is a weeknight dinner dream. It also makes a yummy appetizer bite when cut into small squares.

ACTIVE TIME: 10 MINUTES   **TOTAL TIME:** 25 MINUTES   **MAKES:** 4 MAIN-DISH SERVINGS

1 loaf (about 12 ounces) soft French or Italian bread

2 tablespoons olive oil

1¼ cups shredded part-skim mozzarella cheese

1 package (10 ounces) frozen chopped spinach, thawed and squeezed dry

8 ounces reduced-fat cream cheese (Neufchâtel), softened

⅓ cup fat-free Greek yogurt, or light sour cream

⅓ cup freshly grated Parmesan cheese

2 garlic cloves, crushed with garlic press

¼ teaspoon salt

¼ teaspoon ground black pepper

1 package (9-ounces) frozen artichokes, thawed, patted dry, and chopped

1 lemon

Snipped chives, for garnish

1 Preheat oven to 400°F. Cut bread in half lengthwise, then cut each piece in half across. With hands, press bread to flatten. Line large cookie sheet with foil.

2 Arrange bread, cut sides up, on prepared pan. Brush with oil and sprinkle with 1 cup mozzarella. Bake 5 to 7 minutes or until cheese melts.

3 In large bowl, stir together spinach, cream cheese, yogurt, Parmesan, garlic, salt, and pepper until combined. Divide mixture among pieces of bread, spreading evenly. Top with artichokes and remaining ¼ cup mozzarella. Bake 12 to 18 minutes or until golden brown.

4 Grate peel of half of lemon over pizzas. Garnish with chives.

....

EACH SERVING: ABOUT 645 CALORIES, 32G PROTEIN, 61G CARBOHYDRATE, 31G TOTAL FAT (14G SATURATED), 67MG CHOLESTEROL, 1,245MG SODIUM.

GRILLED TOMATO AND BASIL PIZZAS

Garden tomatoes and basil make a wonderful topping for pizza cooked over the coals. For the crust, use frozen bread dough or fresh dough from the supermarket or pizzeria. For photo, see page 106.

ACTIVE TIME: 30 MINUTES   **TOTAL TIME:** 1 HOUR   **MAKES:** 4 PIZZAS

1   pound (1 piece) frozen bread dough, thawed (from 2- to 3-pound package)

2   tablespoons olive oil

4   ripe medium tomatoes (about 1½ pounds), sliced

4   ounces fresh mozzarella cheese, sliced, or 1 cup shredded Fontina cheese

½   teaspoon salt

½   teaspoon ground black pepper

1   cup loosely packed fresh basil leaves, chopped, plus additional leaves for garnish

1 Prepare grill.

2 Cut thawed bread dough into 4 pieces. On oiled cookie sheet, spread and flatten 1 piece of dough to ⅛-inch thickness. Lightly brush dough with some oil. On same cookie sheet, repeat with another piece of dough. Repeat with another oiled cookie sheet and remaining pieces of dough. For easiest handling, cover and refrigerate dough on cookie sheets until ready to use.

3 Place 1 piece of dough at a time, greased side down, on grill over medium-low heat. Grill until dough stiffens (dough may puff slightly) and grill marks appear on underside, 2 to 3 minutes. Brush top with some oil.

4 With tongs, turn crust over. Quickly top with one-fourth of tomatoes and one-fourth of cheese. Cook pizza until cheese melts and underside is evenly browned and cooked through, 4 to 6 minutes longer.

5 With tongs, transfer pizza to cutting board. Sprinkle pizza with ⅛ teaspoon salt and ⅛ teaspoon pepper. Scatter one-fourth of chopped basil on pizza and garnish with basil leaves. Drizzle with some oil, if you like. Serve immediately.

6 Repeat with remaining dough and toppings.

....

EACH SERVING: ABOUT 495 CALORIES, 18G PROTEIN, 63G CARBOHYDRATE, 20G TOTAL FAT (7G SATURATED), 34MG CHOLESTEROL, 1,175MG SODIUM.

TIP

Subbing soy cheese for the mozzarella in this recipe turns it vegan.

BROCCOLI STIR-FRY WITH
Rice Noodles

Inspired by our favorite Thai noodle dishes, this dish incorporates colorful fresh vegetables and herbs into a lime-spiked coconut sauce. Asian fish sauce is available in the international aisle of the grocery store or in Asian specialty markets.

ACTIVE TIME: 30 MINUTES   TOTAL TIME: 50 MINUTES   MAKES: 4 MAIN-DISH SERVINGS

- 3 limes
- 8 ounces dried flat rice noodles (about ¼-inch wide)
- 2 tablespoons vegetable oil
- 1 bag (16 ounces) broccoli flowerets
- 3 medium carrots, peeled and each cut lengthwise in half, then crosswise into ¼-inch-thick slices
- 2 heads baby bok choy (about 6 ounces each), cut crosswise into 1-inch-thick slices
- 1 cup light unsweetened coconut milk (not cream of coconut)
- 2 tablespoons brown sugar
- 3 tablespoons reduced-sodium soy sauce
- 2 tablespoons Asian fish sauce
- ¼ teaspoon crushed red pepper
- 3 garlic cloves, crushed with garlic press
- 1 tablespoon grated, peeled fresh ginger
- 1 cup loosely packed fresh basil and/or mint leaves, coarsely chopped

1 From limes, grate 1 teaspoon peel and squeeze ¼ cup juice.

2 In large saucepot, heat *3 quarts water* to boiling over high heat; remove saucepot from heat.

Place noodles in water; soak until softened, 6 to 8 minutes. Drain noodles; rinse under cold running water and drain again. Set aside.

3 Meanwhile, in deep nonstick 12-inch skillet, heat 1 tablespoon oil over medium-high heat until hot. Add broccoli, carrots, and ¼ cup water; cover and cook, stirring once or twice, until vegetables are tender-crisp, about 7 minutes. Add bok choy to skillet and cook, uncovered, just until vegetables are tender, 3 to 4 minutes. Transfer vegetables to bowl.

4 In small bowl, combine *⅔ cup water*, coconut milk, sugar, soy sauce, fish sauce, crushed red pepper, and lime juice; stir until blended.

5 In same skillet, heat remaining 1 tablespoon oil over medium-high heat until hot. Add garlic, ginger, and lime peel; cook, stirring, 30 seconds. Add coconut-milk mixture; heat to boiling. Stir in noodles and vegetables; heat through.

6 Transfer to warm serving bowl. Toss with basil and/or mint to serve.

EACH SERVING: ABOUT 420 CALORIES, 11G PROTEIN, 70G CARBOHYDRATE, 13G TOTAL FAT (4G SATURATED), 0MG CHOLESTEROL, 1,215MG SODIUM.

CAULIFLOWER Mac and Cheese

This baked mac n' cheese hides cauliflower and carrots in the cheese sauce, making it both a perfect meal for picky kids and a cauliflower-cheesy vegetable indulgence for adults.

ACTIVE TIME: 30 MINUTES **TOTAL TIME:** 1 HOUR 15 MINUTES **MAKES:** 6 MAIN-DISH SERVINGS

1 head (1½ pounds) cauliflower, core discarded, flowerets cut into 2-inch pieces

4 medium (10 ounces) carrots, thinly sliced

1 cup unsalted vegetable broth

¼ cup reduced-fat cream cheese (Neufchâtel)

1 teaspoon Dijon mustard

1 pinch ground red pepper (cayenne)

¾ cup shredded Gruyère cheese

½ teaspoon salt

½ teaspoon pepper

12 ounces elbow macaroni

8 ounces (3 cups) small broccoli flowerets

2 medium plum tomatoes, cored, seeded, and chopped

¼ cup freshly grated Parmesan cheese

1 Preheat oven to 400°F. Heat 8-quart sauce pot of *salted water* to boiling on high.

2 Add cauliflower and carrots to boiling water. Cook 15 minutes or until very tender.

3 Meanwhile, in blender, combine broth, cream cheese, mustard, cayenne, Gruyère, salt, and black pepper. With slotted spoon, transfer vegetables to blender. Puree until very smooth.

4 Add pasta to same sauce pot of boiling water. Cook half the time that label directs; adding broccoli during last minute of cooking. Drain; return to pot. Stir in cauliflower sauce and half of tomatoes. Spread in 2½-quart shallow baking dish. Top with tomatoes and Parmesan.

5 Bake 35 minutes or until golden brown on top and heated through.

....

EACH SERVING: ABOUT 345 CALORIES, 16G PROTEIN, 53G CARBOHYDRATE, 9G TOTAL FAT (5G SATURATED), 25MG CHOLESTEROL, 480MG SODIUM.

TOMATO AND **Cheese Pie**

A savory custard pie that bakes right in the pie plate—with no crust!

ACTIVE TIME: 20 MINUTES   **TOTAL TIME:** 55 MINUTES   **MAKES:** 6 MAIN-DISH SERVINGS

1   container (15 ounces) part-skim ricotta cheese

4   large eggs

¼   cup freshly grated Parmesan cheese

¾   teaspoon salt plus additional for sprinkling

⅛   teaspoon ground black pepper plus additional for sprinkling

¼   cup low-fat milk (1%)

1   tablespoon cornstarch

1   cup packed fresh basil leaves, chopped

1   pound ripe tomatoes (about 3 medium), thinly sliced

1 Preheat oven to 375°F. In large bowl, with wire whisk or fork, beat ricotta, eggs, Parmesan, salt, and pepper until blended.

2 In cup, with fork, stir milk and cornstarch until blended; whisk into cheese mixture. Stir in basil. Pour mixture into 9-inch glass or ceramic pie plate. Arrange tomatoes on top, overlapping if necessary. Sprinkle tomatoes with salt and pepper.

3 Bake pie until lightly browned around edge and center is puffed, 30 to 35 minutes.

EACH SERVING: ABOUT 190 CALORIES, 15G PROTEIN, 10G CARBOHYDRATE, 10G TOTAL FAT (5G SATURATED), 167MG CHOLESTEROL, 515MG SODIUM.

SOUTH-OF-THE-BORDER
Vegetable Hash

A savory combination of classic hash ingredients (without the meat) gets a new flavor twist from kidney beans, cilantro, and fresh lime.

ACTIVE TIME: 20 MINUTES   **TOTAL TIME:** 50 MINUTES   **MAKES:** 4 MAIN-DISH SERVINGS

3 large Yukon Gold potatoes (about 1½ pounds), cut into ¾-inch pieces

2 tablespoons olive oil

1 large onion (12 ounces), cut into ¼-inch pieces

1 medium red pepper, cut into ¼-inch-wide strips

3 garlic cloves, crushed with garlic press

2 teaspoons ground cumin

¾ teaspoon salt

1 can (15 to 19 ounces) red kidney or black beans, rinsed and drained

2 tablespoons chopped fresh cilantro

plain yogurt, lime wedges, salsa, and toasted corn tortillas (optional)

1 In 3-quart saucepan, combine potatoes and enough water to cover; heat to boiling over high heat. Reduce heat to low; cover and simmer until potatoes are almost tender, about 5 minutes. Drain well.

2 Meanwhile, in nonstick 12-inch skillet, heat oil over medium-high heat until hot. Add onion, red pepper, garlic, cumin, and salt and cook, stirring occasionally, 10 minutes. Add drained potatoes and cook until vegetables are lightly browned, 5 minutes longer. Stir in beans and cook until heated through, about 2 minutes longer. Sprinkle with chopped cilantro.

3 Serve vegetable hash with yogurt, lime wedges, salsa, and corn tortillas, if you like.

EACH SERVING WITHOUT ACCOMPANIMENTS: ABOUT 360 CALORIES, 12G PROTEIN, 63G CARBOHYDRATE, 8G TOTAL FAT (1G SATURATED), 0MG CHOLESTEROL, 625MG SODIUM.

Lo Mein WITH TOFU, SNOW PEAS, AND CARROTS

We've sped up the process of this classic noodle stir-fry by using ramen and sauce.

ACTIVE TIME: 15 MINUTES   TOTAL TIME: 30 MINUTES   MAKES: 4 MAIN-DISH SERVINGS

2 packages (3 ounces each) Oriental-flavor ramen noodle soup mix

2 teaspoons vegetable oil

1 package (14 to 15 ounces) extra-firm tofu, patted dry and cut into ½-inch cubes

6 ounces snow peas, strings removed and each cut diagonally in half (about 2 cups)

3 green onions, trimmed and cut into 2-inch pieces

1½ cups shredded carrots

½ cup bottled stir-fry sauce

3 ounces fresh bean sprouts (about 1 cup), rinsed and drained

1 In 4-quart saucepan, cook ramen noodles (reserving flavor packets) 2 minutes. Drain noodles, reserving ¼ *cup noodle water.*

2 Meanwhile, in nonstick 12-inch skillet, heat oil over medium-high heat until very hot. Add tofu and cook, stirring occasionally, until lightly browned, 5 to 6 minutes. Add snow peas and green onions; cook, stirring frequently (stir-frying), until vegetables are tender-crisp, 3 to 5 minutes. Stir in the carrots, stir-fry sauce, and contents of 1 flavor packet to taste (depending on salt level of sauce) and cook until carrots are tender, about 2 minutes. (Discard remaining flavor packet or reserve for another use.)

3 Reserve some bean sprouts for garnish. Add noodles, reserved noodle water, and remaining bean sprouts to skillet; cook, stirring, 1 minute to blend flavors. Sprinkle with reserved bean sprouts to serve.

EACH SERVING: ABOUT 375 CALORIES, 18G PROTEIN, 47G CARBOHYDRATE, 12G TOTAL FAT (3G SATURATED), 0MG CHOLESTEROL, 1,485MG SODIUM.

MOROCCAN-SPICED SWEET POTATO *Medley*

A spicy combination of vegetables cooked with bulgur and sweetened with dark raisins makes for a one-dish weeknight wonder.

ACTIVE TIME: 20 MINUTES   **TOTAL TIME:** 50 MINUTES   **MAKES:** 4 MAIN-DISH SERVINGS

2   teaspoons olive oil

1   medium onion, sliced

2   garlic cloves, crushed with garlic press

1½ teaspoons ground coriander

1½ teaspoons ground cumin

1   teaspoon salt

¼   teaspoon ground red pepper (cayenne)

1½ pounds sweet potatoes (about 2 medium), peeled and cut into ¾-inch pieces

1   can (14½ ounces) stewed tomatoes

1   cup bulgur (cracked wheat)

2¼ cups water

1   can (15 to 19 ounces) garbanzo beans, drained and rinsed

½   cup dark seedless raisins

1   cup loosely packed fresh cilantro leaves, chopped

plain low-fat yogurt (optional)

1   In nonstick 12-inch skillet, heat oil over medium heat until hot. Add onion and cook, covered, stirring occasionally, until tender and golden, about 8 minutes. Add garlic, coriander, cumin, salt, and ground red pepper and cook, stirring, 1 minute.

2   Add the potatoes, tomatoes, bulgur, and water; heat to boiling over medium-high heat. Reduce heat to medium-low; cover and simmer until potatoes are fork-tender, about 20 minutes. Stir in beans, raisins, and cilantro; heat through. Serve with yogurt, if you like.

EACH SERVING: ABOUT 525 CALORIES, 16G PROTEIN, 109G CARBOHYDRATE, 5G TOTAL FAT (1G SATURATED), 0MG CHOLESTEROL, 1,080MG SODIUM.

TIP

Skip the dollop of yogurt to make this recipe vegan.

Photography Credits

James Baigrie: 25

Mary Ellen Bartley: 28

Brian Hagiwara: 16, 77, 78, 91, 98, 103, 119, 122

iStockphoto: 40; 1 design, 63; Erdosain, 79; Mark Gillow, 45 (carrots); Robyn Mac, 21; Pjohnson1, 45 (potato); Dirk Richter, 90; Syolacan, 117; Alasdair Thomson, 67; Vkbhat, 105; Yin Yang, 83, 121

Rita Maas: 15

Kate Mathis: 6, 10, 31, 38, 41, 81, 86, 97, 104, 110, 116

Johnny Miller: 2, 55 (pizza bagels), 92, 113, 124

Con Poulos: 19, 65

Alan Richardson: 109

Kate Sears: 50

Shutterstock: Andrii Gorulko, 9; hawkeye978, 55 (butcher block); Yuliya Rusyayeva, 45 (onion)

Ann Stratton: 35, 42, 47, 58, 62

Studio D: Julia Cawley, 12; Philip Friedman, 7

Mark Thomas: 21, 74, 106

Anna Williams: 22, 32, 61, 71, 84

FRONT COVER: Johnny Miller (pizza), Shutterstock/marekuliasz (butcher block)
BACK COVER: Ann Stratton

Metric Conversion Charts

The recipes that appear in this cookbook use the standard United States method for measuring liquid and dry or solid ingredients (teaspoons, tablespoons, and cups). The information on this chart is provided to help cooks outside the U.S. successfully use these recipes. All equivalents are approximate.

METRIC EQUIVALENTS FOR DIFFERENT TYPES OF INGREDIENTS

STANDARD CUP (e.g. flour)	FINE POWDER (e.g. rice)	GRAIN (e.g. sugar)	GRANULAR (e.g. butter)	LIQUID SOLIDS (e.g. milk)	LIQUID
¾	105 g	113 g	143 g	150 g	180 ml
⅔	93 g	100 g	125 g	133 g	160 ml
½	70 g	75 g	95 g	100 g	120 ml
⅓	47 g	50 g	63 g	67 g	80 ml
¼	35 g	38 g	48 g	50 g	60 ml
⅛	18 g	19 g	24 g	25 g	30 ml

USEFUL EQUIVALENTS FOR LIQUID INGREDIENTS BY VOLUME

¼ tsp	=							1 ml
½ tsp	=							2 ml
1 tsp	=							5 ml
3 tsp	=	1 tbls	=			½ fl oz	=	15 ml
		2 tbls	=	⅛ cup	=	1 fl oz	=	30 ml
		4 tbls	=	¼ cup	=	2 fl oz	=	60 ml
		5⅓ tbls	=	⅓ cup	=	3 fl oz	=	80 ml
		8 tbls	=	½ cup	=	4 fl oz	=	120 ml
		10⅔ tbls	=	⅔ cup	=	5 fl oz	=	160 ml
		12 tbls	=	¾ cup	=	6 fl oz	=	180 ml
		16 tbls	=	1 cup	=	8 fl oz	=	240 ml
		1 pt	=	2 cups	=	16 fl oz	=	480 ml
		1 qt	=	4 cups	=	32 fl oz	=	960 ml
						33 fl oz	=	1000 ml = 1 L

USEFUL EQUIVALENTS FOR DRY INGREDIENTS BY WEIGHT

(To convert ounces to grams, multiply the number of ounces by 30.)

1 oz	=	¹⁄₁₆ lb	=	30 g
2 oz	=	¼ lb	=	120 g
4 oz	=	½ lb	=	240 g
8 oz	=	¾ lb	=	360 g
16 oz	=	1 lb	=	480 g

USEFUL EQUIVALENTS FOR COOKING/OVEN TEMPERATURES

	Fahrenheit	Celsius	Gas Mark
Freeze Water	32° F	0° C	
Room Temperature	68° F	20° C	
Boil Water	212° F	100° C	
Bake	325° F	160° C	3
	350° F	180° C	4
	375° F	190° C	5
	400° F	200° C	6
	425° F	220° C	7
	450° F	230° C	8
Broil			Grill

USEFUL EQUIVALENTS LENGTH

(To convert inches to centimeters, multiply the number of inches by 2.5.)

1 in	=			2.5 cm	
6 in	=	½ ft	=	15 cm	
12 in	=	1 ft	=	30 cm	
36 in	=	3 ft	= 1 yd	=	90 cm
40 in	=			100 cm	= 1 m

Index

Note: Page numbers in *italics* indicate photos.

THE GOOD HOUSEKEEPING
TRIPLE-TEST PROMISE

At *Good Housekeeping*, we want to make sure that every recipe we print works in any oven, with any brand of ingredient, no matter what. That's why, in our test kitchens at the **Good Housekeeping Research Institute**, we go all out: We test each recipe at least three times—and, often, several more times after that.

When a recipe is first developed, one member of our team prepares the dish, and we judge it on these criteria: It must be **delicious**, **family-friendly**, **healthy**, and **easy to make**.

1 The recipe is then tested several more times to fine-tune the flavor and ease of preparation, always by the same team member, using the same equipment.

2 Next, another team member follows the recipe as written, **varying the brands of ingredients** and **kinds of equipment**. Even the types of stoves we use are changed.

3 A third team member repeats the whole process **using yet another set of equipment** and **alternative ingredients**. By the time the recipes appear on these pages, they are guaranteed to work in any kitchen, including yours. **We promise**.